GW01035560

Basic Buddhism

Basic Buddhism

Sunthorn Plamintr

BUDDHADHAMMA FOUNDATION
BANGKOK, THAILAND

Basic Buddhism

Sunthorn Plamintr

© 1997 **Buddhadhamma Foundation**
All Rights Reserved

ISBN: 974-7890-67-4

First Published by the Buddhadharma Meditation Centre, Hinsdale. Ill.,
as *Basic Buddhism Course* by Phra Sunthorn Plamintr, 1986

Buddhadhamma Foundation
87/126 Tesabahl Songkroh Rd., Lad Yao, Chatuchak, Bangkok, 10900, THAILAND
Tel : (66-2) 589-9012 Fax : (66-2) 974-4791

Printed at
Sahadhammika Co., Ltd.
54/67, 68, 71, 72 Jaransanitwong 12 Rd., Tha Phra, Bangkok 10600, THAILAND.
Tel. (66-2) 8640434-5, 4125887, 4125891 Fax. (66-2) 4123087

Contents

FOREWORD

This book originated from simple lesson sheets that I used while working as a Buddhist Sunday School instructor in the United States some ten years ago. It was originally meant for children of expatriot Thais living in the US, and thus has a marked Thai accent, but it may be used by anyone, even adults, as a simple introduction to the religion. It remains primarily for children, however, and the questions at the back are intended for use in a Sunday School situation.

Since it first appeared in book form, under the title of *Basic Buddhism Course*, in 1986, it went into five editions under that title, a fact that is a source of considerable satisfaction to the author. In this sixth edition, thoroughly revised and improved, I hope that the reader will find a useful introduction into Buddhism.

I am indebted to Bruce Evans of the Buddhadhamma Foundation for his efforts in revising the work—an extensive task which included not only the new title but the addition of four new chapters (8, 9, 10 and 11 of Part I), additions to some of the original chapters, and re-designing the book. Bruce was also responsible for seeing the book through all stages of its production

I would also like to thank the Buddhadhamma Foundation for their interest and support in bringing out this new edition for the benefit of the reading public.

Sunthorn Plamintr
March, 1996

Pali Reading Guide

The transliteration system adopted in this book accords with the standard recognized by the Pali Text Society and other internationally accepted authorities. Variations, however, exist, and these are shown in the table below, in brackets immediately after their Thai counterparts. Not all Roman and Thai letters bear exact Pali phonetic equivalents and they are best learned from a teacher well-versed in all three systems.

Vowels

a	ā	i	ī	u	ū	e	o
อ (ะ)	อา	อิ	อี	อุ	อู	เอ	โอ

Consonants

Gutturals:	k	ก	kh	ข	g	ค	gh	ฆ	ṅ	ง (ŋ, ṁ)						
Palatals:	c	จ	ch	ฉ	j	ช	jh	ฌ	ñ	ญ						
Cerebrals	ṭ	ฏ	ṭh	ฐ	ḍ	ฑ	ḍh	ฒ	ṇ	ณ						
Dentals	t	ต	th	ถ	d	ท	dh	ธ	n	น						
Labials	p	ป	ph	ผ	b	พ	bh	ภ	m	ม						
Others	y	ย	r	ร	l	ล	v	ว(w)	s	ส	h	ห	ḷ	ฬ		
	ṁ	ํ (——ง)														

Examples

Namo Tassa Bhagavato Arahato Sammā Sambuddhassa

(บาลี) นโม ตสฺส ภควโต อรหโต สมฺมาสมฺพุทฺธสฺส

(ไทย) นะโม ตัสสะ ภะคะวะโต อะระหะโต สัมม๋าสัมพุทธัสสะ

Surāmerayamajjapamādaṭṭhānā veramaṇī sikkhāpadaṁ samādiyāmi

(บาลี) สุราเมรยมชฺชปมาทฏฺฐานา เวรมณี สิกฺขาปทํ สมาทิยามิ

(ไทย) สุราเมระยะมัชชะปะมาทัฏฐานา เวระมะณี สิกขาปะทัง สะมาทิยามิ

For non-Thai readers, the pronunciation of some of the main Pali letters roughly goes as follows:

a as in about; ā as in hard; e as in bend; i as in hit; ī as in machine; u as in put; ū as in rude; c as in cello; v as the letter 'w'; ṁ and ṅ as in ring.

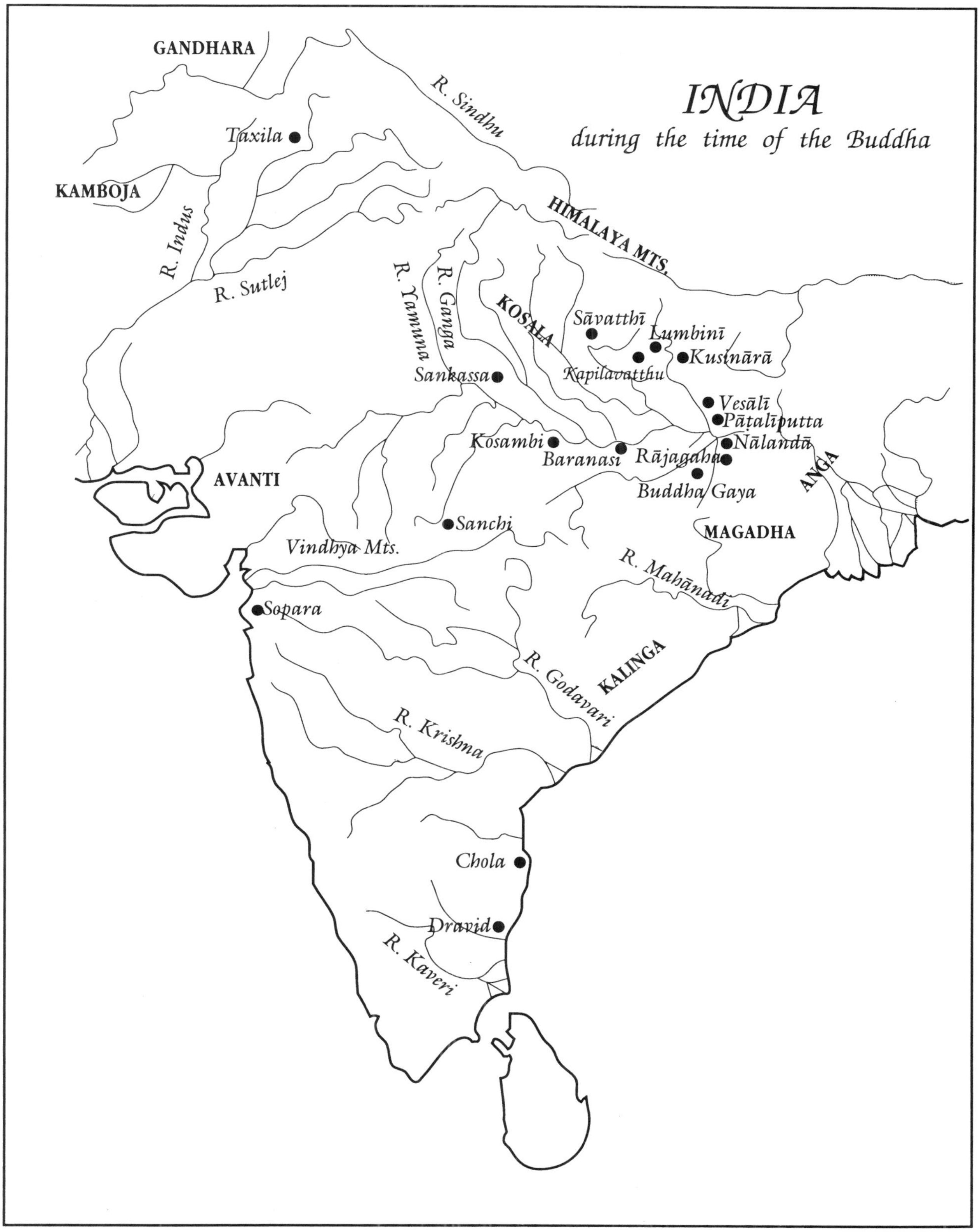
INDIA
during the time of the Buddha
GANDHARA
KAMBOJA
Taxila
R. Sindhu
R. Indus
R. Sutlej
HIMALAYA MTS.
R. Yamuna
R. Ganga
KOSALA
Sāvatthī
Lumbinī
Kusinārā
Kapilavatthu
Sankassa
Vesālī
Pāṭalīputta
Nālandā
Kosambi
Baranasi
Rājagaha
Buddha Gaya
ANGA
AVANTI
MAGADHA
Sanchi
Vindhya Mts.
R. Mahānadī
Sopara
KALINGA
R. Godavari
R. Krishna
Chola
Dravid
R. Kaveri

PART I
THE BUDDHA

1

OUR RELIGION

Buddhism is a very old religion, more than 2,500 years old, founded by the Buddha, who lived in India in the sixth century B.C. India is known as the birthplace of Buddhism because it was from there that Buddhism arose and spread to other parts of the world. We are Buddhists because we practice Buddhism, the teaching of the Buddha.

Buddhism is a religion of self-help. It teaches us to depend on ourselves, to be

courageous and confident in our own abilities. Buddhist philosophy places human beings at the center of all things; it teaches us to strive and work hard to achieve our goals, material or spiritual, through our own efforts, not through prayer or mere wishful thinking.

Buddhism is a religion of free thought. It discourages blind faith and urges us to think freely. It believes in human potential and teaches that all people are capable of attaining the highest state of spiritual liberation. Buddhism also teaches that all people are born equal and are free to choose whatever is best for themselves.

Buddhist teachings are logical and scientific. Some Buddhist principles can be understood through logical reasoning, others must be realized through practical experience. The teaching of the Buddha, though very old, is still valid and practical and can be followed with advantage by all people of the world.

Buddhism teaches us to be kind and gentle. Buddhists are peace-loving people and have never made war in the name of their religion. Today there is violence everywhere in our society because people are selfish and lack kindness. Unlike Buddhism, some religions have a bloody history and their followers still believe that it is right to make war in the name of their religion. Because of this the world is never truly happy or peaceful, and mankind continues to suffer.

Since Buddhism is a religion of self-help, it is suitable for the independent-minded. Because it encourages free thinking, it enjoys a special place in the hearts of free thinkers. Because its teachings are scientific, it is highly respected by the intellectual. The Buddhist emphasis on peace and loving-kindness makes the religion appealing to peace-loving people the world over.

2

THE TRIPLE GEM

There are three objects of the highest veneration in the Buddhist religion: they are the Buddha, the Dharma, and the Saṅgha. These three are called the Three Gems or the Triple Gem. The name implies that they are very precious. Buddhists regard them with profound love and respect.

The Buddha is the founder of our religion. He is believed by many people, Buddhists and non-Buddhists alike, to be the greatest figure in human history. He lived more than twenty-five centuries ago and his teaching has become one of the greatest civilizing forces ever known to man. The Buddha possessed impeccable virtues and profound wisdom, and was said to be worshipped alike by men and deities. Briefly speaking, his virtues are three: infinite wisdom, perfect purity, and universal compassion.

Buddhists are followers of the Buddha. The Buddha is our Spiritual Father, who gives us spiritual life. Because of this we should always love, respect, and be grateful to him.

The Dharma is the Buddha's teaching. It is the Universal Law that the Buddha discovered and taught to the world. It is the Truth, and because the Dharma is Truth, it must be true, valid, and right at all times and in all places.

The Dharma should be studied, followed and practiced. It should be treated with respect because it is essential for world peace and individual spiritual progress. The Dharma can be practiced by all people, whether Buddhists or not.

The Saṅgha is the Order of the Buddha's disciples. The Saṅgha can be divided into two kinds: the Conventional Saṅgha, meaning the Order of Monks, and the Noble Saṅgha, meaning the community of followers, monks and lay people, men and women, who have experienced insight into the Buddha's teaching and are thus possessed of unshakable faith and impeccable moral conduct. The conventional Saṅgha, the monks, study and practice the Dharma and teach it to lay people. They set good examples in moral conduct and inspire us to do good. We pay respect to the Saṅgha because they lead a moral life and preserve the Buddha's teachings.

The Buddha, the Dharma and the Saṅgha are closely interrelated. All three are essential for the rise and spread of the religion. If there were no Dharma, there would not have been a Buddha, but without the Buddha, the Dharma would not have been discovered and taught. If there were no Saṅgha there would be no-one to preserve and spread the Dharma and the religion would have come to an end with the passing away of the Buddha. The Saṅgha, however, would not have come into existence without the Buddha and the Dharma. In this way the three "Gems" are interrelated and interdependent.

These are the Pali words recited in the worship of the Triple Gem:

1. *Arahaṁ sammā-sambuddho bhagavā, buddhaṁ bhagavantaṁ abhivādemi.*
2. *Svākkhāto bhagavatā dhammo, dhammaṁ namassāmi*
3. *Supaṭipanno bhagavato sāvakasaṅgho, saṅghaṁ namāmi.*

3

THE BIRTH OF THE BUDDHA

"Buddha" is a Pali word. It is not a name, but a title meaning the "Enlightened One" or the "Awakened One." The Buddha's personal name was Siddhattha and his clan name was Gotama. Thus, in his early years he was referred to as "Siddhattha Gotama" (Sanskrit: Siddhartha Gautama). The name "Bodhisatta" is also used to refer to the Buddha during the time before he became enlightened. Nowadays we call him simply "the Buddha."

Long, long ago, in the sixth century B.C., near the Himalayas, was a city called Kapilavatthu. It was the capital of the Sakyans, a tribe of the Aryan race that lived chiefly in the North of India. Suddhodana was their king (*raja*). His chief consort was Mahā Māyā (or simply "Māyā"). They both belonged to the warrior or ruling caste, the highest in the hierarchy of the caste system used in those days. This royal couple was destined to become the parents of the greatest human being ever born—the Buddha.

On the full moon day of the month of Visākha (April-May) in the year 623 B.C., a son was born to them in Lumbini Park near Kapilavatthu. Five days later, amid much rejoicing and celebration, a grand ceremony took place in the palace and the infant was given the name Siddhattha ("Wish-fulfillment"), signifying the fulfillment of his parents' long-cherished dreams and aspirations.

In accordance with the custom of the time, many learned Brahmins were invited to the palace for the naming ceremony. Among them were eight men of exceptional learning. Examining the physical signs of the child, seven of them predicted that he would become either a Universal Monarch or a Buddha. But Koṇḍañña, the youngest, who excelled all the others in knowledge, declared that Siddhattha would definitely renounce the world and become the Buddha.

India in the sixth century B.C. was divided into sixteen states, each with its own ruler and government. The subcontinent was rich and prosperous, and rivalry among the more powerful states for economic and political supremacy was common, at times erupting into military struggle and war. It was a time of advanced civilization and spiritual unrest. Brahmanism was the dominant force, but other philosophical systems were also being developed. People were engaged in spiritual pursuit, practicing and teaching what they held to be the highest values. It was into such a climate that our Lord Buddha was born and it was amongst such people that he later taught during his mission years.

4

SIDDHATTHA'S YOUTH

Seven days after the birth of Siddhattha, his mother passed away. Buddhist tradition has it that she was reborn as Māyādevaputta in the Dusita heaven. From that day Prince Siddhattha was looked after by his aunt Pajāpatī, Māyā's younger sister, who would one day become the first woman to be admitted into the Order of Nuns.

From his early years, Prince Siddhattha showed signs of being an extremely gifted child. He was exceptionally intelligent and in a short time mastered all the subjects taught to him. Being the son of a royal family, he was specially trained in the arts of

warfare and government administration. Yet he was profoundly compassionate; his love for all beings, great or small, knew no bounds. There were many incidents that took place during his youth indicating that he was destined to be great. The prophecies were not, after all, given in vain.

One story that illustrates the young prince's great compassion and profound wisdom concerned the Buddha's cousin Devadatta, who one day shot down a bird with an arrow. Siddhattha, seeing that the bird was only injured, not dead, took it and saved its life. An argument arose between them over the possession of the injured bird. They were cousins, but they were very different: Siddhattha was kind and generous; Devadatta was cruel and mean. The argument was earnest and neither side was prepared to give in.

Devadatta argued that he should have the bird since it was he who had shot it down. Siddhattha, on the other hand, argued that the bird should belong to the one who saved it. At the royal court the verdict was passed in favor of Siddhattha.

At the age of sixteen, Prince Siddhattha married Yasodharā, a beautiful princess of the same age from a neighboring state. King Suddhodana wanted his son to succeed him to the throne and become a Universal Monarch, as had been predicted, so he made every effort to ensure that he would be attached to the household life. Siddhattha was accordingly provided with everything he could want and his life as a youth was luxurious, as is fitting for a popular crown prince.

Thus, the young couple lived blissfully unperturbed by the vicissitudes of life outside the palace gates.

5

THE GREAT RENUNCIATION

By nature, Siddhattha was inquisitive and contemplative. In spite of being surrounded by all kinds of luxury and attention, the young prince was not really happy. He sensed that all the sensual pleasures in the world were superficial and impermanent. He wanted to find real happiness for himself as well as for all mankind.

As time passed on, Siddhattha's mind turned toward the problems and mysteries of life. His boundless compassion would not permit him to enjoy the pleasures

of a royal household. He knew no sorrow, but he felt deep pity for suffering humanity. Amidst comfort and luxury he perceived the universality of suffering.

One day, on a visit to the royal pleasure grove, he came across four sights: an old man, a sick man, a corpse, and a wandering monk. The first three sights convinced him of the inexorable fact of change and the universal sickness of humanity. The fourth one suggested to him a way out. From that moment on Siddhattha was more resolved than ever to renounce the worldly life and find true peace and happiness in his own way.

About the same time a son was born to him, who was named Rāhula ("Fetter," or "Obstacle"), but then the time was also ripe for him to depart. With firm determination to discover the Truth and Peace that would benefit mankind, and knowing that his wife and child would be well provided for in his absence, he left the palace to take on the holy life and become a wandering monk, homeless and penniless, with only a few pieces of clothing to cover himself.

He was then twenty-nine years old, still very much in the prime of life. It was a momentous sacrifice that came to be known as the Great Renunciation. Because of this venture undertaken by Siddhattha almost 2,600 years ago, the world today is still endowed with the rich and great spiritual heritage known as Buddhism.

6

THE SEARCH AND THE ENLIGHTENMENT

Prince Siddhattha, now an ascetic, roamed from place to place, sleeping mostly in forests or thick jungles and eating only what was offered him by the local people. He visited several spiritual teachers for instruction and discussion, but soon found their knowledge to be either imperfect or wrong. He knew that such knowledge could never lead him to the Ultimate Truth. Notable among these teachers were Ālāra Kālāma and Uddaka Rāmaputta, who taught Siddhattha very high states of absorption concentration. These were considered great achievements in those days, but even these were not the way to enlightenment that Siddhattha was searching for.

So he began to make experiments on his own. Ascetic practices, such as fasting, eating only fruits fallen from trees, wearing only bark clothing or clothes made from owls' feathers, were a popular way of practice in those days, generally believed to lead to salvation. He tried the most difficult practices and almost died in the process, but the result was no better than the past experiences. Still he did not give in. Instead, he began to reexamine his past efforts to find a new and better method that would finally overcome the spiritual ills of the world. All these experiments and practices took six long years.

During this period of austerities and hardships, Siddhattha was attended by a group of five ascetics, headed by Koṇḍañña, the sage who had predicted that the infant Prince Siddhattha would one day become a Buddha. They all believed that through severe self-mortification the prince ascetic would certainly achieve the goal of enlightenment. They also hoped that if Siddhattha attained enlightenment they would be the first to learn the way from him.

Seeing, however, that he had finally given up the practice of self-mortification and turned instead to pure meditation practice, they thought he had given up the practice. They lost faith in him and decided to part company, leaving the determined Bodhisatta all alone in the wilderness among the jungle beasts.

One night, as he was seated under a Bodhi tree on the bank of the River Nerañjara in an area now known as Bodh-Gaya (Buddha-Gaya), meditating with his mind concentrated and purified, Siddhattha finally developed the supranormal knowledge that destroys all kinds of passions and mental defilements, and he achieved penetrative insight into all phenomena in their true state. The Bodhisatta at last became fully enlightened: he had become the Supreme Lord Buddha.

To attain enlightenment means to gain intuitive insight into reality, thus destroying all mental impurities.

With enlightenment, Siddhattha the Prince was no longer a Bodhisatta (one who is destined to become a Buddha), but the Buddha, the Enlightened or Awakened One, superior to all other beings in wisdom and spiritual attainments. The day of his enlightenment was the full moon in May (Visākha). He was then exactly thirty-five years old.

7

THE FIRST SERMON

The Truth that the Buddha realized is universal. In Buddhist terminology it is called Dharma (Sanskrit) or *Dhamma* (Pali). The Buddha's realization of the Dharma was the result of a long and arduous spiritual quest. He attained enlightenment through his own efforts, without any help from a teacher.

After the enlightenment, the Buddha remained for seven weeks in the vicinity of the Bodhi tree, reflecting on the Truth he had discovered. It became clear to him that what he had realized could not be easily understood by ordinary people, shrouded in ignorance (*avijjā*) and overcome by hatred and lust, so he was at first reluctant to teach the Dharma to the world, fearing that the attempt would be futile. His boundless compassion, however, caused him to reconsider when he saw that people were of different levels of intellect and perfection. Those who had "less dust in their eyes," that is, they were not too ignorant or spiritually blind, would be able to "see" the Dharma and benefit from it, and so he decided to begin his noble mission to teach the world the way out of ignorance and suffering.

The Buddha then started out for Benares (Varanasi) in search of the five ascetics. When they saw the Buddha approaching, the ascetics said to each other, "Look here comes that softy Siddhattha, who gave up the practice. If he wants to sit, let him sit, but we will not rise to greet him." As the Buddha approached them, however, his calm bearing and radiant demeanor overcame them, and they found themselves unable to keep their resolve. One rose to receive him, one went to fetch water, one prepared a seat for him. Even so, they still addressed him as "friend."

"Do not address me as 'friend,' venerable ones," said the Buddha, "I am a Buddha, I have found the Deathless. Take heed, I will teach you the Dharma." However, the ascetics were still not convinced. Three times he spoke to them thus and still they did not believe him. It was only when the Buddha asked them, "Have you ever known me to speak like this?" that they reflected, and realized that the Buddha had never spoken in such a way before and may indeed have become enlightened.

Then, there at the Deer Park near the city of Benares, on the full moon of the month Āsāḷha (June-July), the Buddha delivered the first sermon, which came to be known as the Dhammacakkappavattana Sutta, or "The Discourse on Setting into Motion the Wheel of Dharma." The name of the sermon symbolizes the beginning of a spiritual movement that would permanently affect the religious history of the world.

The first sermon begins with advice against the two extremes that should not be practiced by monks. These are sensual indulgence and self-mortification. The Buddha, having had experience in both, knew that they would not lead to spiritual perfection and enlightenment, and were thus inappropriate for the holy life.

The path that the Buddha advised is called the Middle Way or Noble Eightfold Path. It consists of eight factors: Right Understanding, Right Thought, Right Speech, Right Action, Right Livelihood, Right Effort, Right Mindfulness, Right Concentration.

Briefly, the first sermon states the following:

1. There is "*dukkha*" (suffering)
2. Dukkha is caused by craving (*taṇhā*)
3. There is an end of *dukkha*
4. The Noble Eightfold Path is the way leading to the end of *dukkha*

The Pali word "*dukkha*" has no exact English equivalent. It combines many meanings and connotations, such as suffering, unsatisfactoriness, emptiness, stress, and pain. It is, nonetheless, the word that precisely describes the real nature of existence.

The four points in the first sermon are collectively called the Four Noble Truths. They are the embodiment of all the Buddha's teachings.

8

THE BIRTH OF THE SAṄGHA

The five ascetics who listened to the first sermon were Koṇḍañña, Vappa, Bhaddiya, Mahānāma, and Assaji. Of these, Koṇḍañña was the first to realize the Truth after the Buddha. He is thus considered the Buddha's first disciple.

When the Buddha had finished giving the first sermon, Koṇḍañña achieved the "Eye of Dharma," the special insight into the true nature of things that signified his entrance into the clan of "Noble Ones." Thus he became one of the Noble Saṅgha.

The word Saṅgha means group, community or order, and it is used in Buddhism to connote two special kinds of groups. The first is the group of Noble Ones, those who have experienced either full or partial enlightenment. These may be monks or lay people, men or women, old or young: the only qualification for membership into the Noble Saṅgha is the special quality of mind that is insight into the truth.

People who have realized the truth will naturally do no evil actions, as they have seen the harm of selfishness. Thus, members of the Noble Saṅgha will also possess natural morality (*sīla*), more or less depending on their level of enlightenment. This kind of Saṅgha is called the Noble Saṅgha.

The other meaning of the word Saṅgha is the Order of monks (or *bhikkhus*). Anyone who ordains as a monk automatically becomes a member of the Saṅgha. This kind of Saṅgha is sometimes called the Conventional Saṅgha.

The Conventional Saṅgha, the monks, are also possessed of moral discipline, as they are required by the rules of the Buddhist monkhood to maintain it, but until they are enlightened their morality, not being based on insight, is more or less forced. The Conventional Saṅgha, however, has fulfilled the invaluable service of preserving the Buddha's teachings. It is also the field within which the Noble Saṅgha is most likely to arise. That is, the life of the monks is the one most conducive to practicing the Buddha's teachings and thus it is the most favorable environment within which people can become enlightened.

When Koṇḍañña heard the First Sermon and obtained the Eye of Dharma, he became the first member of the Noble Saṅgha. After hearing the Discourse, he asked for acceptance by the Buddha as a disciple, and when the Buddha accepted him as a *bhikkhu* he became the first member of the Conventional Saṅgha.

9

THE SAṄGHA GROWS

The remaining members of the Group of Five quickly gained insight, and after the Buddha gave the Discourse on Not-self all five became completely enlightened beings (*Arahats*).

Soon afterwards a young man named Yasa, son of a wealthy merchant, was having a party in his father's mansion with many young female musicians to entertain his friends. Late in the night, they all fell asleep. Yasa awoke in the dead of night and, seeing the female musicians, who usually looked so alluring, sprawled out, drooling, snoring, their arms and legs akimbo, he was reminded in the dim light of a graveyard strewn with corpses, and was stricken with a deep sense of the impermanence and emptiness of pleasure seeking. Half delirious, he ran out of his mansion and into the forest, where the Buddha happened to be staying.

Yasa stumbled along, muttering, "Here there is trouble, here there is confusion." The Buddha, hearing him from where he was sitting in meditation, spoke out in a loud, clear voice, "Here there is no trouble, here there is no confusion. Come, listen to the Dharma." Curious, Yasa approached the Lord and after hearing a teaching was enlightened and asked to become a monk under the Buddha. Later, many of Yasa's friends followed to see what had become of their friend, and they too were inspired and enlightened by the Buddha's teaching, and they, too, asked to become monks.

Soon afterwards some young men were going on a picnic with their wives. One of them was not married, so he took along with him a young "lady of pleasure" who he had hired to entertain him. While they were bathing in a river, the young lady made off with their valuables and jewelry. When they realized what had happened, the young men set off in search of her. Seeing the Buddha, they asked, "Did you see a young lady pass by here?" Instead of answering their question, the Buddha asked them, "What is more important: to find a young lady or to find your-

selves?" The Buddha had aroused their curiosity and once more the men were inspired to hear some teaching. They also became monks under the Buddha.

Thus the order of monks gradually grew. When the Buddha converted the three Kassapa brothers, who were well-known ascetic teachers of the time, each with a following of hundreds, the Order of monks swelled, in the first year, to over a thousand.

Thus over the years the Saṅgha spread out and, with the growing numbers, became more formalized. Many of the monks in the Buddha's time were enlightened.

10

THE ORDER OF NUNS

For the first five years of the Buddha's dispensation there were only male monks, *bhikkhus*, in the Order. When the Buddha's father, King Suddhodana, died, the Buddha's aunt and foster-mother, Mahāpajāpatī Gotamī, approached the Buddha and asked permission to be accepted as a female monk (*bhikkhunī*). Three times the Buddha refused permission, whereupon Mahāpajāpatī, with head shaved and wearing ochre robes, and accompanied by a great number of other women, followed the

Buddha on foot from the town of Kapilavatthu to Vesālī, a distance of about 300 kilometers, to plead with him for acceptance. Venerable Ānanda, the Buddha's personal attendant, listened to their plea and approached the Buddha on their behalf. At first the Buddha refused their request, but when Ānanda asked him, "Lord, are women who go forth from the home life to the state of homelessness capable of realizing enlightenment?" the Buddha replied that they were. On being asked once again by Ānanda, the Buddha consented to allow women to be ordained as *bhikkhunī*, female monks.

Mahāpajāpatī Gotamī was the first *bhikkhunī*, and after she and her followers were ordained the Order grew to contain many esteemed *bhikkhunīs*, such as Upalavaṇṇā, Paṭācārā, Soṇā, and Kīsā Gotamī. Their stories make interesting reading. One of them was Bhaddā Kuṇḍalakesā. She was the beautiful young daughter of a treasurer in Rājagaha. Naturally her father had plans for her to marry a suitable young man, but his plans fell apart when one day Bhaddā saw a bandit being led to the execution ground and immediately fell in love with him. She pleaded and pleaded with her father to pay for the criminal's reprieve. Under great pressure from his daughter, the man relented, and his daughter, instead of marrying a suitable young man, married a condemned criminal.

But the man who was her husband had little sense of gratitude. Instead, he plotted to kill his wife and steal her jewelry. On the pretext of wanting to give thanks to the guardian deities, he asked her to take him to the top of the "Bandits' Cliff," from where he intended to take her jewelry and throw her down. However, Bhaddā was a clever woman. She outwitted her bandit husband and threw him off the high cliff instead. Seeing the wiles and fickleness of the sensual world, she became disillusioned with the worldly life and adopted the life of a wandering philosopher. Her wit and wisdom were unrivaled. Wherever she went she would thrust a branch of a jambolan tree into the ground and declare, "Whoever touches this branch must meet my challenge to debate." Her reputation quickly spread as she trounced all who challenged her.

One day she went to the city of Sāvatthī and planted her jambolan branch, announcing her challenge to debate. Venerable Sārīputta was traveling in the area and told one of the local boys to kick the branch over. When Bhaddā saw this she was furious, and went to see Sārīputta and challenged him to a debate. Sārīputta easily answered all her questions, and in return asked her one question, which she could not answer. Inspired by his wisdom, she asked to be a disciple. Sārīputta sent her to the Buddha, and after listening to a teaching she immediately became fully enlightened and took ordination as a *bhikkhunī*. She was said to be the foremost of the *bhikkhunīs* in astuteness.

11

THE BUDDHA'S LAY DISCIPLES

Not all the Buddha's disciples were monks or nuns. From the very early years of the Buddha's mission, lay people from all walks of life were inspired by the Buddha's teaching and the impeccable conduct of the Buddha and the Order. Some of them were kings, such as King Bimbisāra. King Bimbisāra had already been inspired by the Buddha's demeanor when he saw him passing through his kingdom on his quest for enlightenment. Later, when the Buddha, newly enlightened, passed through once again with a company of 1,000 monks, the King went to see him and listened to a teaching, after which he gained insight into the Dharma. King Bimbisāra's faith in the Buddha was so strong that he offered a bamboo grove (Veḷuvana) to the Buddha and the Order to set up the first Buddhist Monastery, and the Buddha spent the second, third and fourth years of his teaching career there.

The Buddha's most well known lay disciples were Anāthapiṇḍika the Merchant and the Lady Visākhā. Both of them had experienced insight into the Dharma through listening to the Buddha's teachings, and both were able to live fulfilling lives amidst the responsibilities of household life.

Anāthapiṇḍika's real name was Sudatta, but he was known everywhere as Anāthapiṇḍika, "Feeder of the Poor," because of his exceptional generosity. During the fifth year of the Buddha's mission, Anāthapiṇḍika, who lived in Sāvatthī, was visiting a friend who was preparing a meal for the Buddha and the Order the following day. The preparations were so lavish that Anāthapiṇḍika thought his friend must have been preparing to entertain the King, but when he was told that he was preparing to offer a meal to the Fully Enlightened Buddha and his company, Anāthapiṇḍika became overwhelmed with joy and determined to go to see the Buddha the very next day.

During his first conversation with the Buddha Anāthapiṇḍika was converted and established unshakable faith in the Triple Gem. He invited the Buddha to spend the Rains at Sāvatthī, and in preparation, bought the forest grove belonging to Prince Jeta. Prince Jeta's grove was a prime piece of land, and he was reluctant to sell it. He said he would only sell it if Anāthapiṇḍika covered the entire forest grove in gold coins. Anāthapiṇḍika proceeded to do so, but by the time he had half covered the grove, Prince Jeta, overwhelmed by Anāthapiṇḍika's unwavering faith, agreed to sell the grove for that amount. The Jetavana Grove became the Buddha's second monastery, and the one at which he spent the most time, twenty-five years in all.

Not all the Buddha's lay disciples were rich or respected. Some were beggars, some were slaves, some, such as the famous Ambapālī, were courtesans. Ambapālī was renowned for her beauty and was the "Lady of the City" for the town of Vesālī. One day she heard that the Buddha would be passing through the area and determined to meet him. She set out with her entourage and invited the Buddha for a meal on the following day. The residents of the town were critical: "How could a prostitute invite the Buddha for a meal at her house?" They tried to dissuade her but she was adamant. Eventually they even tried to "buy" her invitation from her, but she said that she would not trade for the entire city of Vesālī. Ambapālī conceived great faith in the Buddha and offered him a mango grove to make into a monastery. In her later years she ordained as a *bhikkhunī* and became an *Arahat*.

The number of the Buddha's monk and nun disciples was great, but the number of his lay disciples was greater. Thus it is inaccurate to say that Buddhism is a teaching only for people living in monasteries. The Buddha's lay devotees were able to incorporate their understanding of the Dharma into their daily activities and lead more peaceful and fulfilling lives.

12

THE BUDDHA'S CHIEF DISCIPLES

The Buddha had many able and devoted disciples to help him spread his noble teachings. These disciples came from different social backgrounds: there were kings and princes, peasants and laborers, Brahmins and outcasts, teachers, traders, ascetics, actors, prostitutes, and even notorious bandits. Many of them, inspired by the Buddha's teachings, abandoned their earlier ways of life and took up the holy vows, pure and sublime in all respects, and a great number attained the ultimate realization of Truth as did the Buddha.

One of the most well-known of the Buddha's disciples was his attendant, Ānanda. For the last twenty-five years of the Buddha's life Ānanda faithfully attended to his needs, introduced guests to him, followed him on nearly all his journeys, and, most importantly, memorized his teachings. It is largely thanks to Venerable Ānanda that the Buddha's teachings were memorized and later put down in writing. Ānanda was also the monk responsible for persuading the Buddha to accept women into the Order. He was popular among the nuns and was a very gifted teacher.

Mahā Kassapa was another of the Buddha's famous disciples. It was he who convened the First Great Council of monks after the Buddha's passing away to collect and organize the teachings. In addition to his skill in meditation and psychic powers, Mahā Kassapa was known for his faithful observance of the "harder" practices allowed by the Buddha, such as living in the forest, living at the foot of a tree, eating only one meal a day from the alms bowl and using only discarded cloths for robes.

Some of the monks were by nature more reclusive. Venerable Revata, for instance, who was Sārīputta's younger brother, was said to be the foremost of the disciples in keeping to secluded forest dwellings, while Venerable Subhūti was said to be foremost in the development of meditation based on universal goodwill.

All of the foremost disciples were *Arahats*, fully enlightened beings, but each of them had his own tendencies and temperament. All were brought together, however, by the monks' discipline and were one in realization of the Dharma.

Chief among the Buddha's disciples were Sārīputta and Moggallāna. The first was preeminent in wisdom and the second was renowned for his psychic power. The two were close friends since childhood and were even born on the same day.

Moggallāna was born in a village called Kolitagama near Rājagaha (Rajgir), so he was also called Kolita after the name of the village. His father was a rich man and the chief of Kolitagama. His mother was known as Moggali (or Moggallani), from which the name Moggallāna was derived.

One day Sārīputta and Moggallāna went together to the annual festival in Rājagaha. While watching the festivities, the thought struck both of them that all the things they were seeing were only of superficial value and the pleasure they gave was short-lived. Both the performers and the audience would ultimately come to an end. They reflected to themselves:

"Life is impermanent. Sooner or later all people must die. There is no distinction between the rich and the poor, the educated and the uneducated, the high and the low; all must die. This is a fact of life although many tend to forget it. They are afraid of death and hate to think about it. Because of their selfishness they forget the fact that when they came into the world they brought nothing with them, and when they die they can take nothing with them. If people understood this simple truth, they would not be attached to sensual pleasure, but would try to work for higher spiritual happiness."

The two friends decided to renounce the world. They became disciples of Sañjaya, a famous religious teacher of the day. However, they soon became dissatisfied with his teaching because it did not help them to realize their goals. They left Sañjaya and started to roam about, separately, to meet and learn from other teachers. Each promised the other to bring the good news if he found the true doctrine first.

One day Sārīputta came across Assaji, one of the first five disciples who attended on Siddhattha while practicing self-mortification and to whom the Buddha preached the first sermon. Assaji instructed Sārīputta in the fundamentals of the Buddhist philosophy, which he summarized in one single stanza (*gāthā*) as follows:

Ye dhammā hetuppabhavā
tesaṁ hetuṁ tathāgato (āha)
tesañca yo nirodho
evaṁ vādi mahāsamaṇo.

With the mere utterance of this brief stanza, Sārīputta attained the Eye of Truth. Having realized the Truth, Sārīputta hastened to find Moggallāna and repeated to him what he had heard from Assaji. Moggallāna, too, at once attained the Eye of Truth.

The message that the two friends had learned was this:

Whatever things arise from causes, the *Tathāgata* (Buddha) has declared their causes as well as their extinction through the extinction of causes.

This statement describes an important law. It says that everything that exists depends on certain causes. Nothing can take place without causes. When the causes are removed, results will cease to exist. Moreover, those things that are causes themselves are caused by other causes, and so on. All things in the world are thus interrelated and interdependent. This is an irrefutable truth.

This profound teaching holds a valuable lesson for us. It means that if we want good things to happen, we must try to create good causes, and if we want to destroy bad things, we must remove the things that cause them to take place. For instance, if we want to succeed, we must work hard; if we want our friends to love us, we must be nice to them, not selfish.

Because of their conviction in the Buddha's teachings, Sārīputta and Moggallāna sought ordination from the Great Master, who later appointed them as his Chief Disciples. They were both of great help to the Buddha in spreading his noble doctrine and were held in high esteem by the people.

Moggallāna was adept at visiting various other worlds; sometimes he went to heaven and sometimes to hell. He talked to beings in those places and reported his experiences to his followers here, inspiring the people to do good and avoid evil.

The heretical teachers, however, did not like Moggallāna because he attracted so many people, including their disciples. They bribed a gang of brigands to kill the great monk. Moggallāna at that time was living in Kalasila. The murderers surrounded his residence and tried to kill him, but Moggallāna used his psychic powers and escaped unharmed. This happened six times. On the seventh, seeing that he had committed a grave misdeed in a past life and would have to bear its consequences, Moggallāna allowed the thugs to get at him. They fell on him like a pack of wolves, smashing his bones to a thousand pieces, and then left the scene, thinking he was dead.

Moggallāna, somehow, survived. With his great powers, he went to see the Buddha, paid his last homage, and took his leave to die, much to the sorrow of his many followers.

What was Moggallāna's misdeed in the past life?

It is said that long, long ago, in a previous life, he was married to an evil-minded woman who hated his old and blind parents. She wanted to get rid of them and commanded him to kill them. At first the husband would not listen to her, but later he gave in and hatched out an evil plan.

One morning the ungrateful son took his parents in a cart and drove them to the forest. There, unseen by anyone, he left them in the cart. After a while he returned, pretending to be a gang of robbers, shouting and making a great deal of noise. Then he began to beat his blind parents, threatening all the time in a feigned voice. His parents, believing themselves attacked by bandits, shouted to their son to run away.

"Flee, son, flee," they cried. "Bandits are attacking us. Run for your life!"

The old couple loved their son so dearly they did not care for their own lives. Parents are like that. They love and care for their children. There is nothing that can be compared to the love of parents.

Because Moggallāna had committed this grave sin in a previous life he had to suffer the consequences.

13

AṄGULIMĀLA

Aṅgulimāla was one of the best known disciples of the Buddha. His life was a violent one, full of adventures.

Aṅgulimāla was known in his boyhood as Ahiṁsaka or the "Harmless One." His father, Bhaggava, was the court astrologer and chaplain to King Pasenadi of Kosala and his mother was Mantani. He was born in the dead of night under the bandits' constellation.

It is said that at the time of Ahiṁsaka's birth, all the weapons in the city glowed as if on fire, including those that belonged to the king. It was unmistakably an evil omen: the child was destined to become a notorious bloody bandit who would bring destruction and untold terror to his own countrymen.

When he came of age, he was sent to Takkasila for an education befitting the young son of a respectable family. He soon proved to be an excellent student, loved and trusted by his teacher; but he was also an object of envy for his fellow students, who constantly poisoned his teacher's mind against him.

Ahiṁsaka's teacher, thereupon, plotted a scheme to destroy him. He demanded of Ahiṁsaka a tribute of a thousand human lives, each represented by a right-hand finger. This, the teacher hoped, would make Ahiṁsaka a murderer with a price on his head, and would cause him to be hunted down and destroyed.

At first Ahiṁsaka was reluctant to carry out such a bloody mission. He was taught from boyhood to be kind and gentle. He also knew that it was wrong to kill people. But his teacher assured him that once his mission was completed, he would be instructed in a special knowledge that would free him from all wrong and would provide him with great supernatural powers.

Ahiṁsaka thought hard. He did not realize that his involvement with evil people would eventually lead him to an evil path. With great reluctance, he accepted his teacher's demand. He was determined to complete his mission as soon as possible.

The gentle Ahiṁsaka thus became a cruel bandit, merciless and ever bent on killing. He spared none that happened to cross his path, men, women, the aged, and even infants. From each of his victims he cut a finger and tied it to a long string, which he wore around his neck.

Altogether he killed 999 people and the garland he wore had 999 fingers on it. Thus he became known as Aṅgulimāla, the "Finger-Garlanded One."

For years Aṅgulimāla terrorized the countryside and townships. Because of his intelligence and expertise, he was never caught. Villages were deserted and the jungle tracks fell into disuse because the people feared him. King Pasenadi finally ordered a detachment of soldiers to capture him. Dead or alive, Aṅgulimāla had to be caught at all costs.

However, Aṅgulimāla's mother came to know just in time what was going to happen to her son. Determined to save her only son, whom she loved dearly, she hastily made for the jungle where she knew he was hiding in order to warn him. Aṅgulimāla saw his mother coming and, gladdened that the last finger he required would soon be his, rushed forward with raised sword to strike the poor lady who had given him birth and who had raised him up with great love and care.

Before the ultimate crime could be committed, however, the Compassionate Buddha, who had come to know what was going on, appeared before Aṅgulimāla and intercepted him at the last moment.

Like a mad elephant, the bandit turned on the Buddha, who was then walking away. Aṅgulimāla ran after him, determined to finish his task, but however hard he tried he could not come close enough to strike the Buddha with the sword that had tasted the blood of so many human lives.

Miraculously, Aṅgulimāla ran until he was exhausted but could not catch up with the Buddha, who was walking at a leisurely pace. At last Aṅgulimāla stopped. It was the first time he ever had to admit defeat. Still trying to catch his breath, the stone-hearted bandit cried out, "Stop! You there, stop!"

"I have stopped," said the Buddha, still walking, "but you have not."

Aṅgulimāla was puzzled.

"You're lying!" he shouted even louder. "You're walking, but you say you have stopped. I have stopped, but you say I have not."

Came the Buddha's reply: "Aṅgulimāla, I have stopped doing evil. I have also given up running after pleasure. I have given up doing bad deeds, speaking evil speech, and thinking unwholesome thoughts. Come, Aṅgulimāla, listen to the noble doctrine!"

The Buddha then proceeded to deliver a sermon to Aṅgulimāla. Aṅgulimāla was so completely changed by the Buddha's words that he decided then and there to seek admission into the Order. He was later ordained by the Buddha at Jeta Grove, while the angry crowds were yelling at the king's palace for his blood. Little did they know what was going on at the monastery.

Aṅgulimāla's holy life was by no means an easy one. Although he was pardoned by King Pasenadi, who was a staunch supporter of the Buddha, the people did not forget his past misdeeds. When he went outside the monastery, they fell on him with a vengeance, but on the advice of the Buddha he silently endured their wrath and radiated thoughts of love and kindness to them. Gradually, he was able to win their love and respect and, eventually, became one of their most trusted spiritual mentors.

Aṅgulimāla trained himself with great diligence and patience and finally attained Arahantship. His life demonstrates that it is never too late to change oneself for the better.

14

PAṬĀCĀRĀ

Paṭācārā was a *bhikkhunī* disciple of the Buddha. She is one of the best known figures in Pali literature. Her moving life story demonstrates how the Buddha's teaching (Dharma) can help people in distress and provide them with true happiness.

In the city of Sāvatthī there lived a millionaire who had one son and one daughter. His daughter's name was Paṭācārā. She was very beautiful and kindhearted.

Her parents took great care of her and, when she was sixteen, built her a special mansion for comfort and protection and found her a young man of good family and background to whom they expected to give her in marriage.

But Paṭācārā fell in love with a servant and, in order to avoid being married to the man of her parents' choice, decided to elope with her lover.

They ran away to live in a very remote village where they believed her parents would not be able to find them. After some time Paṭācārā became pregnant and began to worry about the safety of her baby. She asked her husband to take her back to her parents, where she would feel secure and would get the best available medical attention.

"It is quite some time since we left my parents. I'm sure they have forgiven us and would be happy to see both of us and our baby," said Paṭācārā one evening.

"What!" exclaimed her husband. "They would tear me to pieces. After what we have done how could they ever forgive me? I wouldn't dare face them. Never!"

"But our child and I could be in serious trouble if I have the baby here," the poor wife pleaded, almost in tears.

The husband pretended to agree to his wife's proposal in order to pacify her, but he kept postponing time after time until her pregnancy became so advanced that Paṭācārā could wait no longer. One day, while her husband was away from home, she set off for Sāvatthī alone.

When the husband returned home in the evening and discovered what had happened, he immediately set off after his wife and overtook her in the jungle, where he found her in labor. Paṭācārā gave birth to a boy with great difficulty. The husband then persuaded his wife to return to their cottage in the village. For some time they lived happily together, forgetting all the hardships and discomforts of life there in the jungle village.

When the first boy could barely walk, Paṭācārā became pregnant once more. Again she asked her husband to take her to her parents, and again he postponed the journey on one pretext or another, until it became plain to Paṭācārā that her pregnancy was too far advanced for her to wait any longer. So she stole away with the first son. Again her husband caught her up while in the jungle and this time, too, the poor wife experienced labor pains just as her husband overtook her.

It was night when this happened, and very dark in the jungle. A storm threatened and before long the rain poured down in torrents. There was darkness all around and the storm raged fiercely.

"Make us a shelter," Paṭācārā cried, "I'm about to give birth!"

The husband hastily went about cutting branches to make a shelter for his beloved wife and child, but alas he was bitten by a poisonous snake and killed instantly, leaving his wife to deliver the second son by herself.

It was very painful for Paṭācārā. She spent the night on all fours sheltering her frightened children, who were constantly crying in fear and discomfort. As soon as it was dawn, she set off to look for her husband, leading the first child with one hand and holding the newborn with another.

What the poor woman discovered filled her with horror and untold sorrow. Great was her grief, and heavy was the burden of responsibility she would have to shoulder. Now there was no turning back. Physically exhausted and emotionally drained, she continued the journey with her two sons until they arrived at the River Aciravati, which was then overflowing due to the heavy rain of the previous night.

"It would be dangerous to cross the river with both boys at once," she thought.

So, leaving the older boy on the bank, Paṭācārā carried the newborn, still red with the stains of labor, to the other side of the river, where she left him on a piece of cloth, and started back to get the older boy. But while she was still in midstream, an eagle spotted the tiny baby and, mistaking it for a piece of meat, swooped down on the poor boy and lifted him up into the air with its powerful claws.

Paṭācārā was horrified. She waved her hands frantically, shouting at the top of her voice against the din of the rushing torrents of the river, but to no avail. Her first son, seeing his mother waving her hands and thinking in his innocent way that she was signaling him to come to her, jumped into the river and was immediately swept away by the relentless current.

Paṭācārā was stunned. Before her very eyes one child disappeared into the empty sky to be killed and devoured by a voracious eagle, while the other was drowned in the river. She stood there, helpless, totally lost and heartbroken.

Great were Paṭācārā's loss and sorrow. She continued her solitary journey, forlorn and desolate. Her only hope now lay with her parents. They were the only people left in the whole world to whom she could turn. On and on she walked. There was no one to talk to; no beloved husband to give her comfort and encouragement, no little children to delight her, and no food to fill her empty stomach. It was quiet all around, frightful and utterly depressing.

As she neared the city, she began to see people. No one recognized her. Everything seemed so strange and unfamiliar. Then she saw a kind-looking man coming her way from the opposite direction and decided to inquire about her parents.

"Please don't ask me about those people," the stranger said, his face suddenly turning sad and uneasy.

"But they are the only people I want to see," insisted Paṭācārā.

"Young lady, don't you know anybody else you want to contact?" asked the stranger, looking straight at her face.

Poor Paṭācārā shook her head.

"Well, then, I'll tell you," said the man after a moment's hesitation. "You know there was a heavy storm last night?"

"Yes, the worst in my life," Paṭācārā's voice was bitter with irony. She could not help feeling apprehensive.

"The rain was so heavy and the storm so fierce the millionaire's mansion collapsed, killing the whole family instantly. Look over there. The smoke is rising high and the fire must still be raging. That is where they are being cremated; the millionaire, his wife, and the son—all three of them!"

Paṭācārā looked at the black smoke. Whatever hope she had previously held seemed to evaporate completely with the smoke. The last blow was so severe she did not know what to do. The poor lady broke into tears, sobbing convulsively.

In one single night Paṭācārā had lost her husband, two sons, parents and only brother. Her tender heart could take it no more. She lost everything, including her senses, and went insane.

Demented Paṭācārā, once beautiful and desired by many wealthy youths, roamed the city streets, naked and emaciated. People made fun of her and the street urchins threw stones and dirt at her. She suffered a great deal. No-one could help her and no-one wanted to.

One day she happened to walk into the Jeta Grove, where the Buddha was teaching the congregation of his followers. Not knowing where she was going, she walked aimlessly into the teaching hall. People were shocked to see a naked young lady walking toward the Buddha and tried to drive her away, but the compassionate Buddha stopped them. With unbounded kindness he spoke to Paṭācārā, radiating the power of his infinite compassion.

"Sister Paṭācārā, come to your senses!" the Lord commanded.

With that Paṭācārā recovered. She regained her sense of shame and suddenly felt uncomfortable to be there in that unbecoming condition. Someone in the assembly threw her a piece of cloth. Then the Buddha taught her about the nature of life, the cycle of birth and death, and how to end it and attain Nirvana. At the end of the sermon she realized the Eye of Truth and asked the Lord Buddha to grant her ordination as a *bhikkhunī*. She worked hard to bring herself further to spiritual perfection and was a great help to the *bhikkhunī* community in which she lived.

One day Paṭācārā was washing her feet; she poured some water on her feet and the water fell to the ground, flowed down a little distance and seeped into the earth. She poured a second time and the water went a little further. The third time, the water went even further before it was absorbed into the sand.

"How like human life it is!" she thought. "Some people die early, some at middle age, some in old age. It is just like water seeping into the ground."

As she meditated, the Buddha appeared before her and uttered the following stanza:

"It is better to live even for one day with discernment of the changeful nature of things than to live a hundred years without it."

At the end of the Buddha's instruction Paṭācārā attained Arahantship. Never before had she felt so happy and free. The Buddha later proclaimed her preeminent among the *bhikkhunī* disciples in the *Vinaya* (Discipline). For many years she helped the Lord spread his noble teaching and passed away at a ripe age.

15

DEVADATTA

Devadatta was the son of King Suppabuddha and Queen Pamitā, who ruled in Devadaha in the North of India. He had a younger sister, called Yasodharā, who was married to Siddhattha. Devadatta was, therefore, Siddhattha's brother-in-law.

Devadatta was also related to Siddhattha in another way. His mother (Queen Pamitā) was a younger sister of King Suddhodana of Kapilavatthu, who was Siddhattha's father. So Devadatta and Siddhattha were also cousins.

Although Siddhattha and Devadatta were related by birth and marriage, they were quite different from one another. Siddhattha was kind, gentle and intelligent. Devadatta was cruel, rough and aggressive. Siddhattha liked to study and meditate. Devadatta was very fond of hunting and games. Siddhattha loved all beings, men or animals, and did not want to hurt or injure any. Devadatta never cared about other beings; he just wanted to have fun and make himself happy, even at the cost of pain for others.

At the age of twenty-nine, Siddhattha left his palace and all worldly possessions to become a monk. Six years later he became enlightened and was known as the Buddha, or the Enlightened One, and he began to teach the Dhamma. The Buddha's teaching spread far and wide and in a short time he gained many followers. People from all social classes flocked around him to hear him teach. They practiced and were benefited by his teaching. They loved and respected the Buddha for he had shown them the right way of living and guided them toward enlightenment. Many men even left home to become monks after him and they helped him to spread his teaching even further.

Devadatta, too, became a monk. At first he was a fairly good monk: he studied the Buddha's teaching and practiced some meditation. As a result he was able to acquire certain psychic powers that enabled him to perform miracles. But by nature Devadatta was self-seeking, conceited and ambitious, so he did not advance very far in his spiritual training.

Devadatta became jealous of the Buddha's fame and influence. He also wanted to be in command of the Order of monks, so he asked the Buddha to resign and appoint him as the head of the Saṅgha. The Buddha, knowing his misdirected ambition and greed, refused to comply. Frustrated, Devadatta decided to kill the Buddha. He knew that as long as the Buddha lived he would never become the head of the Saṅgha.

In order to destroy the Buddha, Devadatta first befriended Ajātasattu, the young prince of Magadha. He wanted to use Ajātasattu in his evil plans. Ajātasattu was not yet the king, so Devadatta urged him to kill his father, King Bimbisāra, who was a staunch supporter of the Lord Buddha, and seize the throne. This Devadatta believed would allow Ajātasattu to use all his influence to annihilate the Buddha. With the Buddha gone, all powers would then fall into his hands.

Ajātasattu was an inexperienced young prince. He believed Devadatta and proceeded to carry out his instruction. King Bimbisāra suffered a great deal before he died at the hand of his own beloved son.

Devadatta's next step was to involve Ajātasattu in his plans to assassinate the Buddha. First he and King Ajātasattu hired a gang of murderers to kill the Buddha, who was then residing on the mountain called the Vulture Peak. Despite their planning and preparation, the effort failed: all the hired murderers changed their minds and became the Buddha's followers.

Devadatta then planned to have the Buddha killed by a killer elephant called Nālāgiri. He told Ajātasattu to intoxicate the animal so it would become mad. In the morning when the Buddha and his monk disciples came into the city, the beast was let loose into the same street, drunk and very fierce. When the people saw the maddened elephant running amuck, they ran helter-skelter to safety as fast as they could and the Buddha and his monks were left to face the danger by themselves.

The Buddha was not, however, afraid of the mad elephant. With the power of his love and purity of mind he was able to calm the animal and make it as tame as a cat. He did not run away, nor did he use weapons. The power of the mind was the only "weapon" that he had. He simply radiated thoughts of love and compassion toward the animal. His power was so great that the elephant was brought to its knees to worship him.

Pure love is a good quality that everyone should develop. In Pali it is called "*mettā*." We should have *mettā* toward all living beings and always wish them happiness and joy. *Mettā* is the opposite of hatred, anger or resentment. The mind that is filled with *mettā* is a happy mind; a society filled with *mettā* is a happy society. A good Buddhist should therefore always practice *mettā* by acting, speaking, and thinking with love and compassion.

Devadatta became more and more frustrated because all his attempts to kill the Buddha had failed. Ajātasattu, on the other hand, had become very unpopular among his subjects. They were angry that he had teamed with the evil Devadatta and had killed his own father, and helped Devadatta to try to destroy the Buddha.

One day Devadatta climbed up the Vulture Peak looking for a good chance to kill the Buddha. He saw the Enlightened One meditating on the walkway below and, seeing that no one was around, moved fast to execute his plan—this time by himself. He selected a huge rock directly above the Lord Buddha and, with the help of a lever, gave it a strong push. The big rock hurtled down the cliff with mighty force, but the power of the Lord was so great that he was only mildly grazed by a stray fragment of the rock. With majestic calm and serenity, he continued to dwell in the bliss of mediation.

A person who does bad things will get bad results. A person who does good actions will get good results. This is the law of karma. This law applies equally to everyone, rich or poor, high or low, young or old. Devadatta did many evil things in his life, so he suffered a great deal before he died. It is said that after his death he was reborn in hell and would continue to suffer there until the force of his evil karma is exhausted.

16

THE GREAT DEMISE

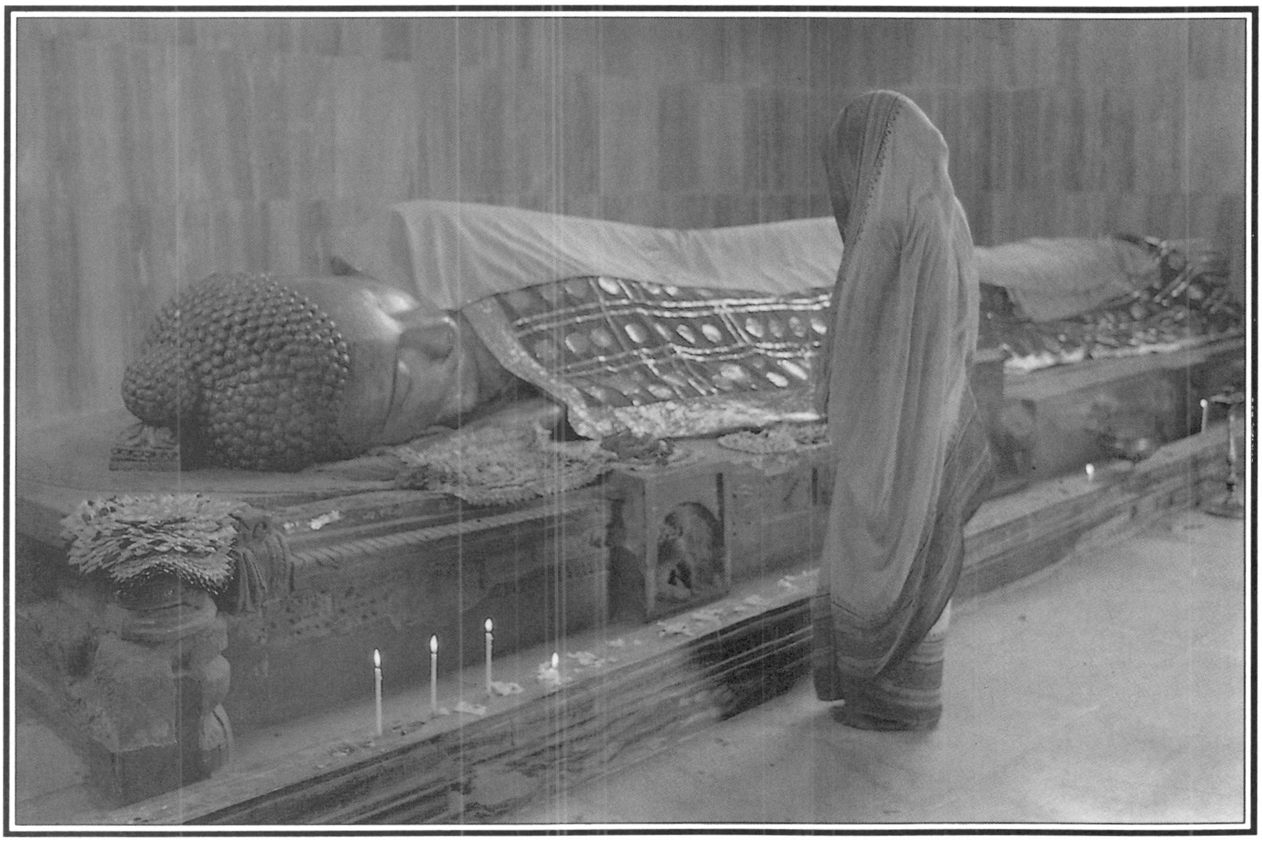

The Buddha worked hard to make people understand the truth and correct social wrongs, and in so doing established a religion that was to become a worldwide spiritual force attracting people in all spheres of life. Many were the problems and obstacles he had to encounter, but he met them all, undaunted, and came out victorious.

Throughout the forty-five years of his teaching career, the Buddha was often on the move, visiting places where he was needed or wherever he felt his presence would be of benefit. Sāvatthī was, however, the city where he spent the most time, twenty-five years, and it was here that most of his sermons were given.

By the time the Buddha was eighty years old the religion had been firmly established and was complete with the "four assemblies of devotees," namely, monks (*bhikkhu*), nuns (*bhikkhunī*), male lay devotees (*upāsaka*), and female lay devotees (*upāsikā*), who would, after his death, be able to carry on the teaching he had begun.

Thus on the full moon of the month of Māgha (February-March) the Buddha informed Ānanda, his personal attendant, that he would pass away in three months from that day. Māgha is the third lunar month, according to the ancient Indian system. The Buddha was to pass away in the sixth lunar month.

The Buddha's prediction of his own death was an important event and came to be known as his "Rejection of the Aggregates of Life." The news spread like wild fire. People were shocked and filled with sorrow; they knew that the Buddha's decision was irrevocable and what he prophesied always came true.

Despite his failing health, the Buddha continued to dedicate himself to the noble task he had undertaken since enlightenment. From Vesālī he went to Kusinārā, a small state to the north, teaching people along the way. The journey was long and painful, but he calmly bore up under the hardships and suffering. Finally, on the full-moon of Visākha, he made it to the Sala Grove, where he was to lay down his worn out frame for eternal rest.

Between two tall sala trees in the grove, Ānanda spread a sheet of cloth for the Buddha. There the Master lay down, physically exhausted, but as ready as ever to teach his followers who were flocking on all sides in order to have a last glimpse of the Lord and hear his last words. It is said that the trees in the grove, though not in season, blossomed in veneration of him, while the assembly sat in respectful silence, shedding tears of sorrow.

The Buddha then gave those present the last opportunity to ask any questions that might be on their minds. No-one did, as all of those present had attained some degree of insight into the teachings and thus had no doubts about the Triple Gem. On this occasion the Buddha also granted ordination to Subhadda, an ascetic of another faith, who sought his audience and who thus became his last disciple.

Then, when the last moment arrived, he gave his last teaching, exhorting his followers to strive ceaselessly for their own salvation (*vimutti*):

"Monks, now I address you: Perishable are all conditioned things. Work out your way with diligence."

With these words, the voice that had woken people from ignorance, delivered the message of universal love, truth, and purity, and brought about a spiritual revolution, became silent. Gone was the guiding light of the world, but all was not lost. The Torch of Dharma that he had lit was passed on to his dedicated disciples who have continued, down the centuries, to carry on the task of the Master.

The passing away of the Buddha is known as the Great Demise or, in Pali, (*Mahā*) *Parinibbāna*. He was then eighty years old. The day was the full moon of Visākha in the year 543 B.C.

It was toward the end of the third watch of the Visākha full moon night, 543 B.C., that the Blessed One passed away. At that moment, the earth is said to have trembled, gods and men were grief-stricken. All were sorrowful, and there was lamentation everywhere, except among the *Arahats*, who were free from all mental defilements (*kilesa*) and had realized Nirvana.

At last the first mournful night at the grove came to a close. When it was light, Venerable Ānanda, himself greatly grieved, went into the city of Kusinārā to inform the people that the Master had passed away. People who heard the news rushed to the Sala Grove and joined the mourning assembly of the Buddha's followers.

The body of the Buddha was kept at the grove for seven days so his followers could pay their last respects. They decorated the place with flowers, garlands, and fragrant materials, and made offerings with music, lights, and other things. The grove was full of people from all directions and walks of life.

On the last day the body of the Buddha was taken out of the grove in a large procession and brought into the city of Kusinārā by the northern gate. The procession paraded through the center of the city and left it by the eastern gate. Then it headed for Makutabandhana Chetiya where the Buddha's body would be cremated. The cremation ground is now considered a sacred site by Buddhists, who visit it in large number every year, for it is here that the physical form of the Buddha rested for the last time before it was consumed by fire.

The news of the Great Demise and the subsequent cremation swept beyond the country to her neighbors. Many kings and rulers wanted to have the Buddha's relics enshrined in their lands so they and their subjects could pay respect to the Master even after he had left. Delegations of envoys were accordingly sent to the Kusinārā court in order to ask for a share of the relics. The rulers of Kusinārā, however, wishing to keep all relics of the Buddha in their land, turned down all those requests.

Displeased by Kusinārā and determined to have their request fulfilled, seven rulers threatened to go to war with the city. These were Ajātasattu from Rājagaha (Rajgir), Licchavi from Vesālī, the Sakyans from Kapilavatthu, Thuli from Allakappa, Koliya from Rāmagāma, Mahābrahmaṇa from Vetthadīpaka, and the Mallas from Pāvā. They all marched their mighty armies to Kusinārā, surrounded it, and prepared to attack.

At that time, there lived in Kusinārā a Brahmin by the name of Dona, who was known for his discretion and fairness. Sensing the destruction that would result from the calamity of war, the wise man addressed the Kusinārā rulers as follows:

"Listen, noble friends! The Lord Buddha, that Supreme Enlightened One, whom we love and respect, taught love and peace to the world all his life. We are his followers, having accepted him, his teaching, and his noble disciples as our guides. Those who have come for his relics are also his followers, having full faith and devotion in him, his teaching and his noble disciples. Let us not go against the Lord's words by quarreling over his sacred relics. Share them in good faith. Let the Lord's glory shine and spread in many lands. That is the least we could do as a gesture of our love and respect for him!"

When the Kusinārā rulers heard Dona's words, they became glad at heart and unanimously conferred on him the responsibility of distributing the Buddha's relics. Dona divided them into eight equal parts, one for Kusinārā and the rest for seven others. All of them built pagodas in their lands to enshrine the relics. The container used to measure the relics was also enshrined in a pagoda constructed for the purpose.

There was another king who came late. He was Moriya of Pipphalivana. He also did not return empty-handed, but received the sacred ashes from the Mallas of Kusinārā. These they enshrined in a pagoda that came to be known as Angarasathupa or the Pagoda of Holy Ashes.

In this way, the relics of the Buddha were distributed and enshrined. It should be remembered, however, that the relics simply serve as reminders of the Buddha's virtues and service to mankind; we do not worship or pray to them as "holy objects" in their own right.

PART II
THE BUDDHA'S TEACHING

1

THE TRIPITAKA

The teachings of the Buddha are classified into three major parts, viz., the *Vinaya*, the *Sutta* (or *Suttanta*) and the *Abhidhamma*. They are collectively called the *Tipiṭaka* or the "Three Baskets."

Tripitaka is a Sanskrit term. In Pali the word is *Tipiṭaka.* "Tri" means three and "pitaka" means basket. Just as a basket is used to contain articles for use when needed, even so each of the three Pitakas contains various discourses of the Buddha delivered during the forty-five years of his mission, as well as a few spoken by his prominent disciples and endorsed by him. The work has its beginning in the First Sermon the Lord gave at the Deer Park two months after his enlightenment.

When the Buddha was alive he was the ultimate authority and he gave the last word on all doctrinal and practical problems in the religion. However, before the Great Demise he did not appoint anyone to succeed him, but indicated instead that the Doctrine (*Dhamma*) and the Discipline (*Vinaya*) he had propounded were to succeed him as teacher.

The Doctrine and Discipline are all in the Tripitaka, and as such the Tripitaka is regarded as the highest authority. We respect the Tripitaka because it contains the words of our great Teacher and is therefore the most reliable guide in religious matters available to us now.

As Buddhists we should therefore try to acquaint ourselves with the Tripitaka and regard it as our guide in religious understanding and spiritual endeavor. We should read it, try to understand it, and put its wisdom into practice in our daily life.

The Vinaya Pitaka or the Basket of the Discipline deals with those rules and regulations formulated by the Buddha for the Orders of *bhikkhus* (monks) and *bhikkhunis* (nuns). They are divided into five major sections and provide a detailed outline for monastic discipline, conduct, and rites. Broadly speaking, they can be compared to the laws and social norms in secular society.

The Sutta Pitaka contains discourses concerning various subjects of wide-ranging significance, social, moral, philosophical and spiritual, and is divided into five major sections. This is the most popular Pitaka since it does not deal with any one specific type of human concern or social group but extends into all social layers and all spheres of human activity.

All the teachings we find in the Vinaya or Sutta Pitakas are rules or discourses that the Buddha made in response to the problems, questions or situations that presented themselves to him. As such they are not detached from life but concern it in a very positive and direct way.

The Abhidhamma deals mostly with the psychological and philosophical aspects of the doctrine. It is the most difficult of the three Pitakas, but is also very important for intellectual discipline and better understanding of the Sutta Pitaka. The subjects taken for deliberation in this Pitaka are what Theravada Buddhism considers to be absolute truths, of which there are four: mind, mental concomitants, matter and Nibbāna (Skt. Nirvana).

The Tripitaka, also known as the Canon, was originally composed in the Pali language and has been transliterated into many forms of script and translated into all major languages of the world. Volume upon volume of commentary and sub-commentary have been written on the Tripitaka and they, too, have been rendered into many languages.

Buddhism was once looked upon by some people as an outdated cult with strange beliefs and practices followed by certain barbarian tribes in the East, but once the Tripitaka and other important Buddhist works were translated into English Westerners were surprised to find many things in the religion that were relevant to the modern world. Some prominent figures in the West have openly admitted the superiority of Buddhist teachings and practices. The great historian H. G. Wells even asserts that the religion "has done more for the advance of world civilization than any other influence in the chronicles of mankind."

2

THE FIRST SERMON

A translation of the Buddha's First Sermon, the Dhammacakkappavattana Sutta, is presented in brief below:

Thus have I heard: Once the Blessed One was dwelling near Benares, at Isipatana, in the Deer Park. Then the Blessed One spoke thus unto the company of five monks:

"These two extremes, monks, should not be followed by one who has gone forth from the world:

"Indulgence in sense pleasures, which is low, vulgar, common, ignoble, and useless, and indulgence in self-mortification, which is painful, ignoble, and useless.

"Avoiding these two extremes, the *Tathāgata* (Buddha) has gained the realization of that Middle Path which produces insight and knowledge and tends to calm, to higher knowledge, enlightenment and Nirvana.

"And what, monks, is that Middle Path which produces insight and knowledge, and tends to calm, to higher knowledge, enlightenment and Nirvana?

"It is this Noble Eightfold Path, namely, Right Understanding, Right Thought, Right Speech, Right Action, Right Livelihood, Right Effort, Right Mindfulness, and Right Concentration.

"This then, monks, is the Middle Path which produces insight and knowledge, and tends to calm, to higher knowledge, enlightenment and Nirvana.

"Now this, monks, is the Noble Truth of Suffering *(dukkha):* Birth is suffering, old age is suffering, sickness is suffering, death is suffering, sorrow, lamentation, pain, dejection, and despair are suffering. Association with undesirable things is suffering, separation from desirable things is suffering. Not getting what one desires is suffering. In short, the Five Aggregates of Attachment are suffering.

"Now this, monks, is the Noble Truth of the Origin of Suffering: It is the craving that leads to rebirth, combined with pleasure and lust, seeking delight here and there; namely, craving for sensual pleasure, craving for existence and craving for nonexistence.

"Now this, monks, is the Noble Truth of the Cessation of Suffering: It is the extinction without remainder of craving, the abandonment, renunciation, release, and non-attachment.

"Now this, monks, is the Noble Truth of the Way Leading to the Cessation of Suffering: it is this Noble Eightfold Path, namely, Right Understanding, Right Thought, Right Speech, Right Action, Right Livelihood, Right Effort, Right Mindfulness and Right Concentration.

"Monks, as to things unlearned before, there arose in me vision, insight, understanding, there arose in me wisdom and light that, 'This is the Noble Truth of Suffering.'

"Monks, as to things unlearned before, there arose in me vision, insight, understanding, there arose in me wisdom and light that 'Indeed, that Noble Truth of

Suffering is to be comprehended.'

"Monks, as to things unlearned before, there arose in me vision, insight, understanding, there arose in me wisdom and light that, 'Indeed, that Noble Truth of Suffering has been comprehended.'

"Monks, as to things unlearned before, there arose in me vision, insight, understanding, there arose in me wisdom and light that, 'This is the Noble Truth of the Origin of Suffering.'

"...there arose in me wisdom and light that, 'This ... Origin of Suffering is to be destroyed.' ...there arose in me wisdom and light that, 'This ... Origin of Suffering has been destroyed.'

"...there arose in me wisdom and light that, 'This is the Noble Truth of the Cessation of Suffering ... the Noble Truth of the Cessation of Suffering should be realized ... the Noble Truth of the Cessation of Suffering has been realized.'

"...there arose in me wisdom and light that, 'This is the Noble Truth of the Way Leading to the Cessation of Suffering... the Noble Truth of the Way Leading to Cessation of Suffering should be developed....'

"Monks, as to things unlearned before, there arose in me vision, insight, understanding, there arose in me wisdom and light that, 'Indeed, this Noble Truth of the Way Leading to the Cessation of Suffering has been developed.'

"So long as in these Four Noble Truths my true knowledge and insight was not perfectly purified in threefold and twelve ways, even so long I would not proclaim the Supreme Incomparable Enlightenment of wisdom in the world with its gods, devils, Brahmas, among its population of recluses, Brahmins, deities and men.

"But when, monks, my true knowledge and insight was perfectly purified in threefold and twelve ways as to these Four Noble Truths, then did I announce attainment of the Supreme Incomparable Enlightenment of wisdom in the world with its gods, devils, Brahmas, among its population of recluses, Brahmins, deities and men.

"Knowledge arose in me, insight arose in me that the release of my mind is total. This is my last existence; now there is no more rebirth."

Thus spoke the Blessed One, and the five monks, gladdened, rejoiced at the Lord's utterance. While this exposition was being uttered, there arose in the Elder Koṇḍañña the pure and stainless Eye of Truth (which made him realize that) whatever arises is liable to disappear.

Thus, when the Wheel of Dharma was set in motion by the Blessed One, the earth-dwelling gods proclaimed: "This supreme Wheel of Dharma has been set in motion by the Blessed One at the Deer Park in Isipatana near Benares, a Wheel which, once set in motion, cannot be stopped by anyone, be they recluse, Brahma god, devil, Brahmin, or anyone else in the world."

(Then follows a description of the proclamation by gods of different heavens up to the Brahma world.)

Thus, at that very time, at that moment, the sound of proclamation went up as far as the Brahma world. This ten-thousand fold world system shuddered, shook, and trembled. Infinite and magnificent light appeared in the world surpassing all the divine majesty of the gods.

Then the Blessed One exclaimed: "Indeed Koṇḍañña has understood. Indeed Koṇḍañña has understood." In this way, Elder Koṇḍañña became known as "Aññā Koṇḍañña" ("Koṇḍañña who has understood").

3

UNDERSTANDING DUKKHA

"Dukkha" is one of the most misunderstood Pali words in Buddhism. It is one of the themes in the first sermon and occurs in many other discourses dealing with the nature of life or existence. The term embraces many meanings and refers to different things in different contexts.

Buddhism has often been criticized for having a pessimistic slant in its world outlook. It has been accused of giving undue emphasis to the unsatisfactory conditions of existence, such as physical suffering, frustration, disappointment, poverty, and disease, and overlooking the pleasurable conditions that are equally available in the world.

Such a criticism is primarily based on a wrong interpretation of the first Noble Truth proclaimed by the Buddha, which attempts to define the nature of the world in realistic terms. It is the Noble Truth of *Dukkha*, popularly, but perhaps misleadingly, translated as "suffering," "unsatisfactoriness," "pain" and similar terms or phrases, each of which carries but a partial implication of the original meaning intended by the Buddha.

It is true that in ordinary usage the word "*dukkha*" means suffering as opposed to the word "*sukha*," which means comfort or happiness, but when it is used in the first Noble Truth to describe the nature of life and the world, the term acquires a much more profound meaning. It signifies deeper concepts such as imperfection, impermanence, emptiness, and insubstantiality.

Buddhism distinguishes three kinds of *dukkha*. The first category, *dukkha-dukkhatā*, includes all mental and physical experiences that are generally considered as unpleasant, undesirable, and painful, such as, sickness, death, misery, poverty, agony, distress, and discomfort. In other words, *dukkha-dukkhatā* means all kinds of suffering in the ordinary sense, to which all living beings are subject. It is the most apparent form of *dukkha* because it can be directly experienced by the senses.

Often it is only this category of *dukkha* that the first Noble Truth is taken to represent, and this gives rise to the misconception that Buddhism is pessimistic in its world outlook.

The second category of *dukkha* is called *vipariṇāma-dukkhatā*, the *dukkha* caused by change. Specifically it is the inherent unsatisfactory nature of happiness, which, since it changes, always leads to suffering.

The Buddha does not deny that happiness exists, nor does he advocate avoiding all pleasures by closing our eyes and ears and pretending to be blind and deaf to all objects around us. The Buddha, however, wants us to realize the limitations and impermanent nature of happiness and pleasure. In the Aṅguttara Nikāya, a volume of the Pali Canon, he distinguishes between happiness based on the senses on one hand, and spiritual bliss, which is independent of material things or sensual desires, on the other. The former is the happiness of sense pleasures and the latter that of renunciation, but all are included in *dukkha*.

The third form of *dukkha* is not the feeling of suffering but the inherent imperfection of all conditioned phenomena *(saṅkhāra-dukkhatā)*. It is the most important aspect of the first Truth. It is identified with the Five Aggregates, namely, physical form, feeling, perception, mental formations, and consciousness, that make up what we perceive to be an "individual," an "I" or "being."

Greed, desire, and attachment are the sources of *dukkha*. We feel unhappy, disappointed and depressed because we are attached to ourselves or our identities. Everything that we experience is related to us and consequently causes in us the dual concepts of like and dislike, good and bad, desirable and undesirable. Our mind is thus influenced by what we experience and loses its freedom. That is why the Buddha says: The five aggregates of attachment are *dukkha (Pañcupādānakkhandhā dukkhā)*. That is, attaching to the physical form, feelings, perceptions, mental formations or consciousness will lead to suffering.

4

THE DOCTRINE OF KARMA

The word "karma" is Sanskrit. Its Pali counterpart is "*kamma.*" (Compare "dharma" and "*dhamma*" in Sanskrit and Pali respectively.) It is derived from the root "kar" meaning "to do" or "to perform." Karma thus means action.

According to the Buddhist doctrine of karma, not all actions are called karma, only those that are performed with intention or volition. Says the Buddha: *Cetanāhaṁ bhikkhave kammaṁ vadāmi* ... Monks, I say that volition is karma."

Karma can be performed through three "doors" or channels:

1. *Kāya-kamma*: Bodily action.
2. *Vacī-kamma*: Verbal action.
3. *Mano-kamma*: Mental action.

An action can be either good or bad; a good action is called *kusala-kamma* and a bad one, *akusala-kamma*. The Pali word "*kusala*" is translated as "wholesome," "skillful," or "meritorious," and "*akusala*" means just the opposite.

Thus *kusala-kamma* means actions that are good, wholesome, skillful, and meritorious and *akusala-kamma* means those that are bad, unwholesome, unskillful, and demeritorious.

We should understand the distinction between the two kinds of actions. In general, we may say that such good actions as giving a helping hand to mother or father at home, being nice to them, being generous, diligent, and truthful are *kusala-kamma*. Such actions as selfishness, rudeness, laziness, disobedience to parents, rude gestures, cruelty, stealing and lying are *akusala-kamma*. The Buddha classified good and bad actions according to the three "doors" through which they are performed, as follows:

10 WHOLESOME ACTIONS

3 Bodily Actions

1. Refraining from killing (or hurting)
2. Refraining from stealing or cheating
3. Refraining from misconduct to persons dear to others (or sexual misconduct)

4 Verbal Actions

1. Refraining from false speech
2. Refraining from slander
3. Refraining from harsh speech
4. Refraining from frivolous speech

3 Mental Actions

1. Non-covetousness, not greedily desiring things belonging to others
2. Goodwill or kindness
3. Right view or understanding

There are also ten unwholesome actions, which are just the opposite to those listed above. Wholesome actions are not merely negative. For example, "refraining from stealing" does not only mean that one should avoid such an act, but also signifies such positive qualities as respect for the property rights of others and right livelihood.

An action, be it good or bad, produces a result. Sometimes the consequences are immediate and explicit; sometimes they are not. However it is always true that good actions produce good results and bad actions bring about bad ones. We should, therefore, try to do good and avoid evil.

5

THE DOCTRINE OF REBIRTH

The problem of rebirth or life after death has been a controversial issue which has attracted the attention of almost all religious teachers since time immemorial. There were those who supported the belief and those who rejected it.

Evidence and explanations both for and against rebirth seem equally convincing, but at no time in all religious history has there been any definite solution to the problem. This is largely because the nature of the issue is such that it defies verification or foolproof logical analysis. Nevertheless, Buddhism has also participated in the discussion of this complicated, time-honored issue and it is worth examining how our religion deals with it.

The Pali word for rebirth is "*punabbhava*," variously and misleadingly rendered as reincarnation, re-existence, re-becoming, or transmigration of the soul. To prevent misunderstanding, it should be noted that Buddhism does not subscribe to the belief in an everlasting, unchanging entity or soul which is supposed to reside in living beings. To be reborn, according to Buddhism, does not mean that a soul leaves its old body and goes to take possession of a new one. The Buddha teaches the doctrine of no-soul; this is Buddhism's point of departure from all other religions.

Buddhism states that everything that exists is subject to change; nothing is permanent or everlasting. Life is a continuum or flux, consisting of the *pañcakkhandhā*, the Five Aggregates, namely, physical form, feeling, perception, mental formations, and consciousness. These five make up what we call a "being" or an "individual," and they are ever in a state of change. In other words, they rise and fall, originate and disappear, in an unending succession, the speed of which is so swift and subtle we cannot ordinarily see it. In this sense, we can be said to undergo an unbroken process of birth and death, i.e., we are "born" and "die," in each and every moment of our lives, and the process continues in the same manner right to the "next life."

Strictly speaking, a person is not, therefore, the same for two consecutive moments. Neither is he different, for the preceding moment gives rise to the next, which again causes the following one, and so on.

When the Five Aggregates arise and fall in the preceding moment, they also lead to the arising of the following set of Aggregates, which in turn produce the next set. This is how life functions and continues to the next birth. Rebirth is thus possible in this way without the intervention of a soul. This is also the reason why Buddhist scriptures say that what is reborn is neither the same nor different.

To say that a man or being is reborn is one extreme, to say that there is no rebirth is another. Buddhism avoids these two extremes. Based on the law of cause and effect, the Buddhist teaching states instead that rebirth is possible and will take place when there are appropriate causes or conditions; it will not take place if no proper causes or conditions are present.

Buddhist scriptures also speak of another kind of rebirth. Unlike the popular concept, this type of rebirth is a mere mental state that keeps changing from one condition to another. We feel happy one moment, unhappy at another. At one time our mind is wholesome and pure, at another it is just the opposite. This change in the mental state constitutes a "rebirth." Thus, we are "reborn" every moment into high or low "births" every time the conditions of our minds change.

Buddhism further asserts that desire or attachment, based on ignorance (*avijjā*), is the principle cause of rebirth, both in this life and the next, and is also the most powerful moving force behind our actions. Like the oil that feeds a lamp, this mental defilement supplies the fuel for the continuation of the cycle of birth and death (*saṁsāra*). Just as a flame dies down and cannot be rekindled once the fuel is spent, the cycle of birth and death naturally comes to an end when all mental impurities are completely destroyed.

Nibbāna or Nirvana is the state of perfect freedom from all mental defilements, attainable through the purification of mind. It is the highest bliss.

Rebirth is thus the result of one's own karma. Wholesome karma leads to a good birth and unwholesome karma leads to a bad one.

6

THE DHAMMAPADA

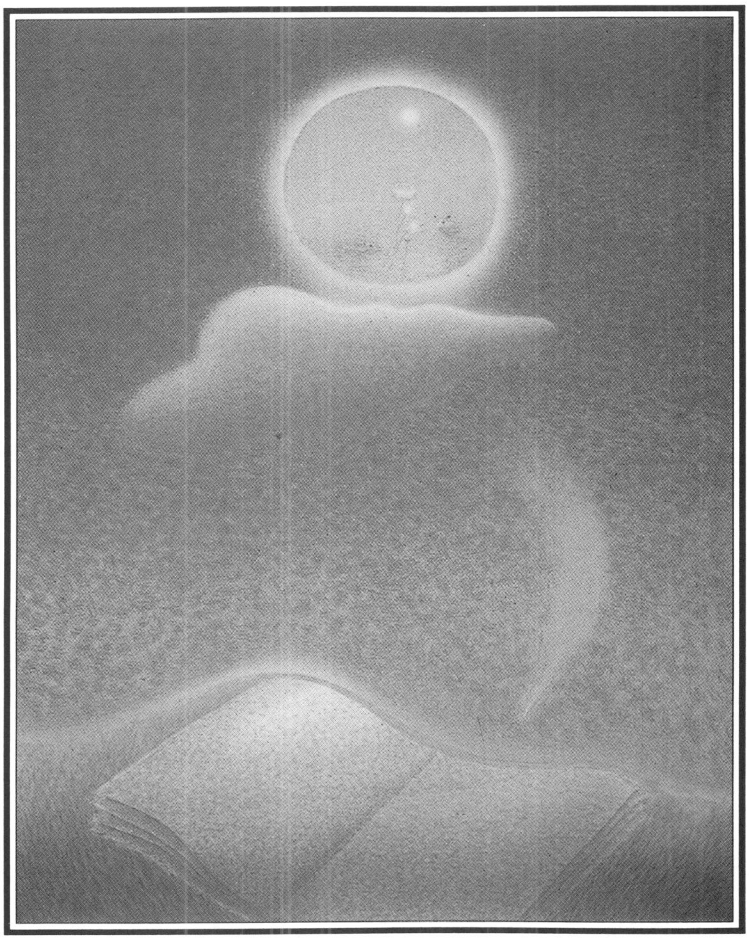

The Dhammapada (meaning "Path of Dharma") is a collection of 423 Pali verses uttered by the Buddha on various occasions to a wide range of audiences. It is probably the best known work in Theravada Buddhist literature. These verses have been collected from different books of the sacred Buddhist literature, the Tripitaka. Each verse is a guideline for happy living. Whoever follows the Dhammapada wisdom will definitely taste the bliss of timeless Dharma.

Here are a few verses selected from this great work, simplified and adapted to facilitate comprehension:

1. Mind is the most important thing, mind is the source of all actions. If we act or speak with an impure mind, suffering follows just as the wheel follows the ox's hoof. If we act or speak with a clean mind, happiness follows like our never departing shadow.

2. Hatred never ceases by hatred, but by love and kindness.

3. Just as rain penetrates through a poorly thatched house, even so does lust break through the uncultivated mind.

4. Hard-working men, ever heedful and alert, outstrip the lazy and careless ones as a swift horse outstrips a weak horse.

5. Ever grows the glory of those who are energetic and mindful, whose deeds are pure and well-considered, who are restrained, righteous, and vigilant.

6. Mind is fickle, unsteady and hard to control, but the wise straighten it as a fletcher fashions his arrow.

7. Good is the taming of the mind, which is difficult to control, flighty and willful. A mind that is well-trained brings happiness.

8. An ill-placed mind brings greater harm than does one's enemy.

9. This body is impermanent and perishable; some day it will lie on earth, devoid of consciousness and useless like a log of wood.

10. The sweet smell of flowers does not blow against the wind, but the fragrance of virtue does. Truly, the virtuous man pervades all directions with the fragrance of his virtues.

11. The fool who realizes his folly may thereby become wise, but the fool who thinks he is wise remains a fool.

12. Foolish (evil) people are their own enemies. They do evil actions that results in unhappiness and pain.

13. As a solid rock is not shaken by the wind, even so do the wise remain unshaken by blame and praise.

14. Irrigators convey water; fletchers fashion the arrow; carpenters fashion wood; good people train themselves.

15. Let one be quick to do good and restrain the mind from evil; the mind of one who is slow in doing good finds delight in evil.

16. Refrain from all evil, do only what is good, purify your mind: this is the ad-

vice of the Awakened Ones.

17. Let one conquer hatred with love and evil with righteousness; let one conquer the miser with generosity and the liar with truthfulness.

18. Good is restraint in action, speech and mind. One should be restrained everywhere. He who is restrained in every way is freed from all suffering.

7

THE MAṄGALA SUTTA

The Maṅgala Sutta is one of the most often-quoted discourses in the Pali scriptures. It contains many practical hints for those who desire a prosperous life and spiritual progress.

The word *"maṅgala"* holds a special appeal because it means blessing, prosperity, or auspiciousness. In almost all Buddhist auspicious ceremonies monks are asked to recite this discourse in order to bring about the favorable effects suggested by its name. It should be noted here that, according to Buddhism, blessings are more the creations of our own action than a result of external factors. This means that if we want to prosper, materially or spiritually, we have to work things out for ourselves, and the Maṅgala Sutta explains what we ought to do in order to achieve this end.

It is said that while the Buddha was staying at the Jeta Grove in Sāvatthī, a question arose among the people there as to what constituted true blessings in life. Different people held different views and no agreement could be reached. According to some, a blessing (*maṅgala*) was a particular sight, such as a pregnant woman, a little boy, or a white bull. Others argued that a blessing was a sound, such as the words "success" and "luck," or the sound of music. There were yet others who asserted that such favorable experiences as smelling the fragrance of flowers or touching the earth were blessings. And so the argument raged on.

All the people who were arguing formed their ideas on the basis of what they could experience with their senses. They thought, for example, that if you heard someone else say the word "luck," "fortune," or "success" then you would eventually be blessed with luck or success. The sight of a pregnant woman suggested to them the idea of fullness or fulfillment, so they thought it would bring them happiness. They were speculating on external factors and did not understand the importance of man's inner quality.

It is said that the debate on blessings was not confined to human beings, but was taken up by deities, who also found themselves unable to decide the issue. One night a certain deity visited the Buddha at his dwelling in the Jeta Grove and put the question to him. Thereupon, the Blessed One delivered what came to be known as Maṅgala Sutta, the Discourse on Blessings.

The Buddha enumerated thirty-eight blessings in the Maṅgala Sutta, graded from the most fundamental to the highest spiritual attainment—Nirvana.

If we carefully examine the thirty-eight blessings we find that each is useful in itself and is directly relevant to our life. The first blessing, for example, tells us not to get involved with evil people or allow ourselves to be influenced by their ways. The second one advises us to associate with good people, for such association brings happiness and prosperity.

The Maṅgala Sutta thus gives us positive guidelines for our lives. If we follow them consistently, we shall progress both materially and spiritually and enjoy a truly happy life. Each blessing makes us more perfect and brings us closer to the final religious goal. Those blessings that are described at the end of the Sutta are closer to spiritual practice and are less concerned with the life of ordinary people, yet they can be practiced, though in lesser degree, even by lay followers.

Here is a translation of the Maṅgala Sutta:

Not to associate with fools (evil ones), to associate with the wise, and to honor those who are worthy of honor—this is a highest blessing.

To reside in a good locality (favorable environment), to have done meritorious deeds in the past, and to set oneself in the right course—this is a highest blessing.

Wide learning, skill, good discipline, and pleasant speech—this is a highest blessing.

Supporting one's parents, cherishing wife and children, and a peaceful occupation—this is a highest blessing.

Generosity, righteous conduct, helping relatives, and blameless actions—this is a highest blessing.

Reverence (to the Triple Gem, parents, elders, etc.), humility, contentment, gratitude and the opportune hearing of the Dhamma—this is a highest blessing.

Forbearance, obedience, seeing *samaṇas* (holy men) and the discussion of Dhamma at proper times—this is a highest blessing.

Self-control, leading the holy life, the "seeing" of the Noble Truths, and realization of Nirvana—this is a highest blessing.

If a man's mind is sorrowless, stainless, and secure, and does not quake when touched by worldly vicissitudes—this is a highest blessing.

Those who thus acting are everywhere undefeated, attain happiness everywhere—to them these are the highest blessings.

8

THE FOUR KEYS TO SUCCESS

All people want to be successful in life, but not everyone meets with success. Successful people are recognized and respected: the stories of their lives are recorded and studied both by their contemporaries and later generations. They are immortalized and looked upon as a source of creative inspiration for those who desire to succeed like they did.

The Buddha taught the way to success in many of his discourses. According to one of these discourses, there are four virtues that, when developed, lead to success and enable man to achieve his goals in life. They are Will, Effort, Application, and Reflection (*Pali: Chanda, Viriya, Citta, and Vīmaṁsā).*

The first key to success is the will to work or to fulfill one's duties to the best of one's ability. This means that one should have desire, interest, and determination to work. Without the will to do something, how can we do it? Will is a positive kind of desire that leads to growth and improvement, thus it is a condition that the Buddha encouraged. Will is, in fact, a primary requirement in the execution of one's responsibilities, and without it nothing much can be accomplished.

The second is effort or perseverance. This implies the ceaseless application of energy to the task required of one. When we undertake to do something we should exert ourselves, fully and continually, until the task is completed. If a student was merely interested in a subject but did not make the effort to study it the chance for success would be very slim. Effort is therefore a very important factor for success. We should try to cultivate this virtue in us.

Application means the ability to control our mind and keep it on the task at hand. If we were digging a garden, for example, but all the time thinking about going to the movies, we would have no concentration on our work, and the job would be done inefficiently and slowly. Whatever we do, be it great or small, we have to apply our thought to it, again and again, until it is finished. We should be positive in our thinking and firm in our goals.

The last virtue is reflection. Reflection is necessary in all kinds of activities. When we work, we should always examine the work we do; we should have good planning and a proper understanding of the work. It is not enough to work hard; we need to reflect on the results of our work, using our intelligence and common sense. A good example of reflection is how the Buddha reflected on the fruits of his ascetic practices and honestly asked himself just what benefit he had achieved from them. When he saw that they led to no benefit and led him no nearer to the truth, he was brave enough to abandon them, in spite of the fact that they were generally considered in those times to be the only way to enlightenment. Only those who work in this way will attain a high degree of success. The use of reflection will prevent us from doing wrong things and ensure our success. It is therefore very important that we learn how to cultivate reflection and use it in all our activities.

9

TWO VIRTUES THAT PROTECT THE WORLD

It is said that human beings are social animals. Living together in a society, we need a body of laws to keep peace and ensure justice for all its members, without which it would be impossible for the society to function. We can say, therefore, that all of us are under the protection of law. But the Buddha taught about a different kind of protection, a far superior one—moral protection.

According to the Buddha there are two virtues that provide us with the best protection. They are:

1. *Hiri* – Shame at doing evil (moral shame)

2. *Ottappa* – Fear of the results of doing evil (moral dread)

Hiri is moral shame or conscience. It arises out of an understanding of what is right or wrong, good or bad, and is developed through a constant application of moral vigilance.

A person with *hiri* does not do anything rashly or without proper forethought, but will exercise caution in all actions. Before doing anything, he wisely asks himself, "Is it right or wrong? Is it good or bad?" If he finds it to be wrong or bad, he will not do it, no matter what the temptation. If, however, he realizes after an unprejudiced consideration that what he intends to do is right and good, he will make an effort to finish the task and not give up.

Hiri can be compared to the feeling a person who loves cleanliness may experience when he sees something loathsome or disgusting. He wouldn't put his hand into a trash bag full of stinking garbage if he could avoid it. If he came across a mud puddle, he would step aside to avoid getting himself and his clothes soiled.

In the same way, a person with *hiri* feels averse to bad actions, be they physical, verbal, or mental, and will endeavor to avoid them as far as possible. He does not do such things as stamping his feet before his parents, talking impolitely back at them, or having an unkind and disrespectful thought toward them, for he knows that by so doing he is only spoiling himself.

Ottappa is moral dread or fear of the consequences of wrong or immoral actions. It is the result of a firm belief in the doctrine of karma which states that a willful action sooner or later brings about an appropriate consequence.

One who has *ottappa* is afraid of doing evil deeds because he knows that they will bring bad results and unhappiness to himself and others; he will not, on the other hand, hesitate to do the right things, firmly believing that the consequences thereof will be pleasant and beneficial. Unfortunately, some people tend to do just the opposite—they are brave when it comes to doing evil, but cowards when it comes to doing good.

Ottappa can be compared to fear of a poisonous snake. Just as a person avoids snakebite, knowing that it is fatal, even so a person with *ottappa* tries to avoid evil because he knows that its consequences are painful. He does not do wrong things even when he is sure that he will not be caught, for he understands that the law of karma operates at all times and all places. For the same reason he is encouraged to do good even if no-one else notices it or acknowledges his good deeds.

If people practiced these two virtues, the world would be well protected and there would be less need for law. No evil deeds would be committed even in secrecy. The world would then be a very happy place for us all.

10

FOUR VIRTUES LEADING TO TEMPORAL WELFARE

Buddhism deals not only with spiritual subjects, like rebirth, but also places strong emphasis on our material needs and immediate problems in this very life. In fact, the emphasis is on this life—*the here and now*—rather than on the next. Do good now, exhorts the Buddha, for no one knows if death will come tomorrow.

There is a discourse in the Aṅguttara Nikāya, one of the Volumes of the Pali Canon, in which Lord Buddha talks about the virtues that are conducive to material benefits in the present. When practiced constantly, these four virtues enable one to succeed in life and attain happiness and prosperity. They are:

1. *Uṭṭhāna-sampadā*—The endowment of energy
2. *Ārakkha-sampadā*—The endowment of vigilant protection
3. *Kalyāṇamittatā*—Association with good people
4. *Samajīvitā*—Balanced life-style

The first virtue, *uṭṭhāna-sampadā,* is the most important quality to begin with. *"Uṭṭhāna"* literally means "to go up" or "to rise." To succeed in life a person must be filled with enthusiasm and energy; he or she must be fired with ambition and a strong desire to succeed, to be the best. Students who are endowed with this quality will make sure that they always obtain good grades, not just aiming to pass the tests. They recognize that education is the foundation of their future life, so they are determined to make the foundation strong by studying hard, and are ever eager to learn more and to the best of their ability.

Only those who work hard will succeed. Greater success requires greater will power. Sometimes in the process of gaining success we have to endure doing things that we do not want to, or being deprived of the pleasures and joys that we would like to have, but the result of such an effort is a good one. So good Buddhists must be energetic and industrious.

Wealth and fortune come to those who work hard, but one cannot get rich if one does not know how to protect or take care of what has already been acquired. For this we must practice the second virtue. The second virtue, *ārakkha-sampadā,* advises us to be vigilant, not careless, about what we have earned or possessed. We must know, for example, how to use our money properly so it will give maximum benefit. Strange though it may seem, many people do not know how to use their money. They waste it on cigarettes, drink and drugs, which only enslave them and drag them toward a premature death, impoverishing them in the process. Many people lose their fortunes in gambling, shamelessly ruining their families; many are forced to crime or illicit occupations and end up in prison. Instances of the lack of *ārakkha-sampadā* are many and so obvious that no further explanation is necessary.

The third virtue, *kalyāṇamittatā,* is no less important for achieving success. People cannot live alone; they need friends, associates, and colleagues (in addition to relatives, of course). These people play a significant role in our lives. They can influence our thought, change our views and character, and even promote or ruin our lives. If you are very close, for instance, to a friend who is foulmouthed, arrogant, and has no respect for his parents, and if you keep company with him long enough, you will gradually imitate his habits. This is one of the reasons why many good students from good families fall for drugs and other bad habits. On the other hand, with good friends, one will be encouraged in good habits which naturally lead to benefit.

Samajīvitā—a balanced life—means a life that is wisely conducted, neither too frugal nor extravagant. It is a Dharmic life, a life that is noble, useful and contented. A person with *samajīvitā* lives according to his means; he is not carried away by the high fashion of the day. His life is exemplary, free from pretensions and harm. It is a life of service rather than of selfishness. Living in this way ensures not only that whatever has been acquired is well protected, but also that whatever is spent is wisely and usefully spent.

11

BUDDHIST MEDITATION

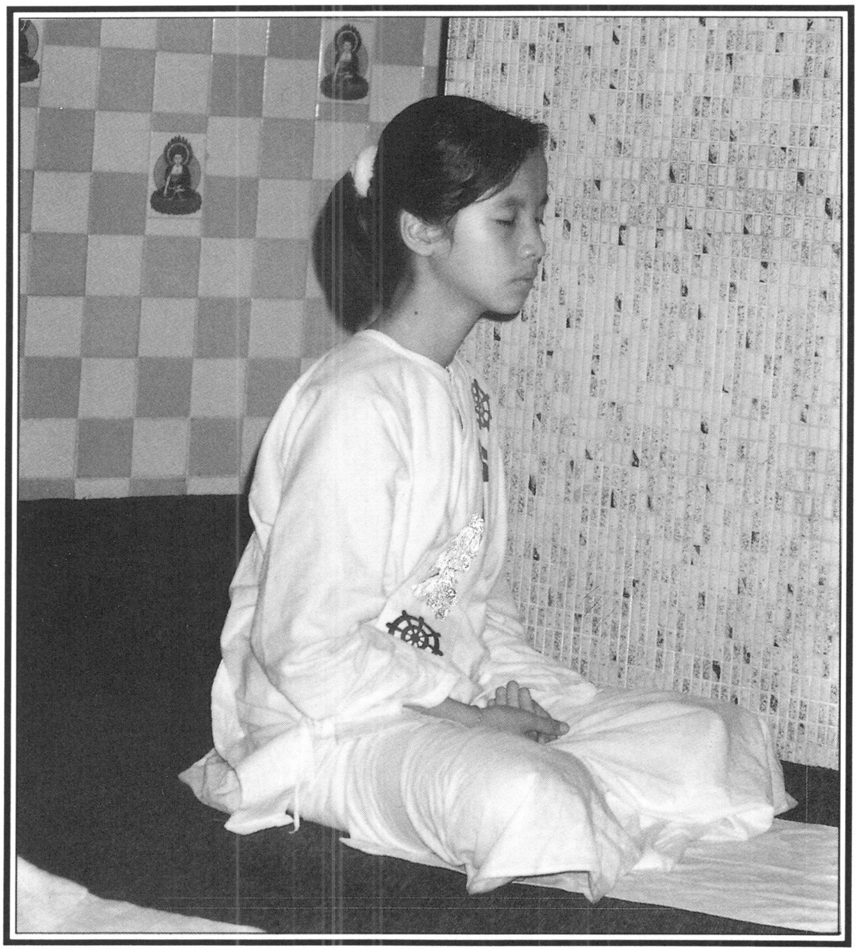

Of the many aspects of the Buddhist teaching, meditation occupies a special place of interest, particularly in the West. In a number of Asian nations, like Thailand, Japan, Sri Lanka, and Burma, where Buddhism is still a very living force, it forms part of a long and uninterrupted tradition, and has received even wider recognition in recent years.

As science and technology become increasingly developed, people have come to realize more and more the relevance and significance of Buddhist meditation. Those who are earnest in its practice and properly understand its nature and application always find their effort more than rewarding.

Meditation is a means to mental development. In Buddhism, mind is considered to be the most important composite of a person's makeup. All the evil and noble deeds that are committed in the world are a result of thoughts. That is why the Buddha repeatedly said that mind is the forerunner of all actions, the chief of all things. Thus the mind should be trained, refined and perfected. Meditation is the way to do this.

Beginners who desire favorable results should be instructed and trained by an experienced teacher who can supervise and guide their progress.

Because meditation is the training of the mind and because mind is the factor that manipulates and controls our actions and speech, the practice of meditation can bring innumerable benefits to our lives, such as those listed below:

1. Meditation helps to calm and organize the mind.
2. Meditation strengthens our will power and enables us to face problems and difficulties with confidence.
3. Meditation helps us to think positively.
4. Meditation improves our efficiency in work by helping us to concentrate better and sharpening our mental faculties.
5. Meditation frees us from worries, restlessness, and other negative influences.
6. Meditation increases our mental health and in so doing has a positive effect on our physical health.
7. Meditation cleanses our mind of defilements (*kilesa*).
8. Meditation encourages virtuous qualities like kindness, inner peace, humility and pragmatism, and prevents us from being influenced by such elements as passion, arrogance, selfishness, hatred, jealousy, or greed.
9. Untrained people are often dominated by delusion (*avijjā*) and their own preconceptions which prevent them from having proper understanding of things. Meditation helps to remove such obstacles.

It should, however, be borne in mind that the degree of benefit a person can derive from meditation depends entirely on the degree of achievement he or she makes and on how far he or she can apply meditation to real life. There are several factors that are important for the success of the practice, such as proper atmosphere, spiritual maturity, proper frame of mind, self-confidence, and frequency and regularity in practice, but, as with other activities in life, trying to do one's best is always better than not trying at all.

Concentration and insight

Buddhism teaches two kinds of meditation:

1. *Samatha-bhāvanā* – Concentration or Calm Meditation
2. *Vipassanā-bhāvanā* – Insight Meditation

Samatha-bhāvanā aims at gaining concentration or one-pointedness of mind and *vipassanā bhāvanā* enables the practitioner to purify the mind and acquire insight into the real nature of phenomena.

Technically speaking, concentration is the basis of insight. It is developed by fixing one's mind on a chosen object, such as a Buddha image, candlelight, a circular colored disc, or the breathing. Buddhist commentaries elaborate forty kinds of meditation objects, but the list may be extended.

Insight meditation, on the other hand, is practiced through the application of one's mind to the nature of things—being constantly mindful of one's physical and mental activities—so that one may thereby penetrate deeply into the real nature of existence and do away with mental impurities. In short, insight meditation is the direct method of cleansing the mind of all evil.

Both concentration and insight meditation can be developed side by side and the development of one helps in the cultivation of the other, but ultimately it is only insight meditation that, when perfected, leads to the highest wisdom and cleanses the mind of all impurities once and for all.

Both kinds of meditation can be practiced and applied to our daily life and both are of immense benefit. Nevertheless, for those who are not acquainted with the practice or have no prior personal experience, the guidance and supervision of an expert teacher is recommended

One of the most popular methods of gaining concentration, practiced widely now in both the East and the West, is concentration on breathing. This is done by focusing the attention on the in- and out-breaths. The point of focus may be the nose-tip or the abdomen as it rises and falls with the breathing. Repeating in one's mind the word *"bud-dho"* (Buddha) as one breathes in and out is another very effective way of developing concentration and is much recommended. It is so easy to practice even a little child could do it, yet it is useful in many ways.

The practical steps are as follows:

1. Sit cross-legged with the right foot on the left one. Use a cushion if necessary. Make the back straight but not tense.
2. Place the right hand on the left, palms upward.
3. Close your eyes, relax the whole body, relaxing every muscle. Free your mind from all worries and cares.
4. Breathe in and out naturally. Mentally repeat "bud" ("u" as in "put") when breathing in, and "dho" when breathing out. Do not think about anything else. When the mind is distracted by thoughts, sounds, or sensations, as it inevitably will be, note them for what they are and bring the attention back to the breath. Try to control your mind as best you can.

The best methods for insight meditation are found in a famous discourse delivered by the Buddha called the Satipaṭṭhāna Sutta, the Discourse on the Foundations of Mindfulness. According to this discourse, there are four objects that may be taken for the practice, namely, Body, Sensations, Mind, and Mental Objects (Pali: *Kāya, Vedanā, Citta, and Dhamma).*

Mindfulness is the key in insight meditation. When practicing this type of meditation, one should endeavor to be mindful of one's activities, mental or physical, at all times. Mindfulness should be developed to such an extent that it becomes natural and automatic. When that stage is reached, one can be said to dwell constantly in mindfulness. This is the way to spiritual purification.

Remember that meditation can be best learned not from a written lesson, but from an experienced teacher.

12

BUDDHA'S FINAL ADDRESS

The following are extracts from the Mahāparinibbāna Sutta, the Discourse on the Great Demise:

When the Blessed One had stayed as long as he wished at Ambapālī's grove, he proceeded to Beluva, near Vesālī. There the Blessed One addressed the monks, saying: "O monks, take up your abode for the rainy season roundabout Vesālī, each one according to where his friends and close companions may live. I shall enter upon the Rains here at Beluva."

When the Blessed One had thus entered upon the Rains there fell upon him a dire sickness, and great pains crushed upon him even as unto death. But the Lord, mindful and self-possessed, bore the pains of sickness in silence and calm.

Then this thought occurred to the Blessed One:

"It would not be proper for me to pass away from life without addressing the disciples, without even taking leave of the Order. Let me now, by strong effort of the will, subdue this sickness again and keep my hold on life until the proper time has come."

And the Lord, by a strong effort of the will, subdued the sickness, and kept his hold on life until the time he fixed upon should come. And the sickness abated.

After the Rains, the Blessed One together with the company made his way by stages to the town of Pāvā. While at Pāvā the Blessed One sat down on a seat spread out in the open air. And Venerable Ānanda, accompanied by many other disciples, approached where the Blessed One was, paid him due homage, and, respectfully taking a seat on one side, said:

"I have beheld, Lord, how the Blessed One was in health, and I have beheld the Blessed One suffer. Though at the sight of sickness of the Lord my body became weak as a creeper, and the horizon became dim to me, and my faculties were no longer clear, yet notwithstanding, I sought some consolation in the thought that the Blessed One would not pass away from existence so long as he had not left instructions concerning the Order."

And the Blessed One addressed Ānanda for the sake of the Order and said:

"What, then, Ānanda, does the Order expect of me? I have taught the Truth without making any distinction between exoteric and esoteric doctrines; for in respect of the Truth, Ānanda, the *Tathāgata* has no such thing as the closed fist of a teacher who holds some things back.

"Truly, Ānanda, should there be anyone who thinks, 'It is I who will lead the Order,' or 'The Order is dependent upon me,' he should then lay down instructions in matters concerning the Order. Now the *Tathāgata* (Buddha), Ānanda, thinks not that it is he who should lead the Order, or that the Order is dependent upon him. Why, then, should the *Tathāgata* lay down instructions in matters concerning the Order?

"I am now grown old, Ānanda, and full of years. My journey is nearing its end. I have come to the sum of my days, turning eighty years of age. Just as a worn-out cart can be made to move on only with much difficulty, so the body of the *Tathāgata* can only be kept going with much additional care.

"Ānanda, it is only when the *Tathāgata,* ceasing to attend to the outward, becomes absorbed in that deep meditation of heart, having no concern with bodily object, it is only then that the body of the *Tathāgata* is at ease.

"Therefore, monks, be ye lamps unto yourselves. Rely on yourselves; rely not on external help. Hold fast to the Truth as a lamp. Seek salvation alone in the Truth. Look not for assistance to anyone beside yourselves.

"And how, Ānanda, can a monk be a lamp unto himself, rely only on himself and not on any external help, holding fast to the Truth as his lamp and seeking liberation in the Truth only, not looking for it from anyone beside himself?

"Herein, Ānanda, let a monk, as he dwells contemplating on the body, so regard the body that he, being full of effort, thoughtful and mindful, may, while in the world, overcome the pain that arises from the body's cravings.

"While subject to sensations, let him so regard the sensations that he, being full of effort, thoughtful and mindful, may, while in the world, overcome the pain that arises from the sensations.

"And so, too, when he thinks, reasons or feels, let him so regard his thought that, being full of effort, thoughtful and mindful, he may, while in the world, overcome the pain that arises from the craving due to ideas, reasoning, or feeling.

"Those who, either now or after I am gone, shall be a lamp unto themselves, relying upon themselves only and not relying upon any external help, holding fast to the Truth as their lamp, and seeking their liberation only in the Truth, not looking for help from anyone beside themselves, it is they, Ānanda, among my *bhikkhus,* who shall reach the very topmost height! But they must be glad at heart to learn..."

Having eaten the morning meal at Pāvā, the Blessed One journeyed on to nearby Kusinārā. There, in the forest of Sala trees, the Blessed One lay down on his right side and spoke his last words to the Order:

"Monks, now I address you. Perishable are all conditioned things. Work out your way with diligence."

PART III
BUDDHIST PRACTICE

1

WHY WE STUDY BUDDHISM

There are many good reasons why we should study Buddhism; some are quite explicit while others become clear only after earnest deliberation. The following are some of the more significant reasons:

1. Buddhism is our religion and is therefore a vital part of our lives. It gives us an identity and relates us to one of the most powerful civilizing forces in the history of mankind. Whatever we do, we should always strive to do as well as we can, and to

be good Buddhists we should first study Buddhism.

2. Buddhism is one of the most important sources of world civilization. It is said that even the Christian faith in its early days may have been greatly influenced by the Buddhist teaching. Buddhism is time-tested, more than 2,500 years old, enjoys worldwide acceptance, and is regarded with respect by intellectuals throughout the world.

3. In terms of physical wants and needs, human beings do not basically differ from animals; both need food, shelter and rest. Both need protection and care. Most of our actions are intended to satisfy these physical needs; the difference lies only in the ways we find them. It is religion that elevates human beings above the physical

plane and gives them a totally different dimension. When we study Buddhism, we learn how to rise beyond animal instincts and find satisfaction in the spiritual realm. We learn how to make our life more meaningful than it would be otherwise, and to become true human beings.

4. Buddhism is the most scientific and practical of religious teachings, and that is why more and more knowledgeable people are turning toward it. Buddhist doctrine (Dharma) helps prevent those who study and practice from falling prey to

superstition and false beliefs. During the time of the Buddha people held many unskillful beliefs and practices, such as the caste system, animal and human sacrifices and self-mortification—to name a few—but the Buddha denounced them all. He fought hard against those harmful practices and taught the noble doctrine. Many of those who believed in him became enlightened and free. We should, therefore, study the religion so we, too, may benefit from his wisdom.

5. During the forty-five years of his mission, the Buddha gave countless discourses. These discourses contain invaluable advice and practical guidance which can be applied to our everyday life. In fact, they are meant to be practiced, not simply believed.

Let us take, for example, the Buddha's advice: Depend on yourself. This simple teaching is undoubtedly true and realistic. It teaches us to be strong, to take responsibility for our own actions and to be brave in facing their consequences. It is so true and reasonable that no one in his right mind would argue otherwise. If only people followed this advice, the world would be a much happier place to live in.

6. All Buddhists should consider it their duty not only to practice the religion, but also teach it to others. We must work hard to preserve and spread the noble doctrine of the Buddha. To share the Dharma is, indeed, a very great merit. As the Buddha said, "The gift of Dhamma excels all other gifts." Naturally, one can share the Dhamma only when one has studied it.

2

BEING A BUDDHIST

There are three things that are most important to Buddhists, namely, the Buddha, the Dharma, and the Saṅgha.

The Buddha is the founder of the Buddhist religion, the Dharma is his teaching, and the Saṅgha is the Order of enlightened disciples, who preserve and propagate the religion. Buddhists regard these three things as the objects of the highest veneration. Collectively, they are called the Triple Gem.

To be a Buddhist means to take refuge in the Triple Gem—to have firm faith in the Buddha, the Dharma, and the Saṅgha—and to endeavor to follow Buddhist practices and traditions.

One can take refuge in the Triple Gem by making a firm resolution to that effect, with or without accompanying rites or ceremony, and by calling oneself a Buddhist. After all, Buddhism is a religion that lays great emphasis on actual practice—one must follow the teaching and conduct oneself accordingly—not on ritual trappings or elaborate ceremonies that bear no ethical or spiritual value.

Nevertheless, since Buddhism has also become institutionalized, there has evolved a traditional practice which we may call the Confirmation Ceremony, by which a person may be officially "confirmed" or recognized as a Buddhist. This ceremony is usually officiated by a member of the Order and there is a procedure that has to be properly followed.

First of all, an aspirant wishing to become a Buddhist should be taught the basic tenets of the religion. He should study the fundamental teachings of the Buddha, what a Buddhist should or should not do, how a Buddhist should behave in relation to others, how he should behave in a Buddhist congregation, and so on. He should also learn how to pay homage and respect to the Triple Gem and how to observe the five precepts, which are the fundamental moral codes of conduct for all Buddhists.

In the confirmation ceremony and in the presence of a member (or members) of the Order one should recite the following passage: *Esahaṁ bhante, suciraparinibbutampi, taṁ bhagavantaṁ saraṇaṁ gacchāmi, dhammañca, bhikkhusaṅghañca, buddhamāmakoti saṅgho maṁ dhāretu, anukampaṁ upādāya. Dutiyampi, esahaṁ bhante... Tatiyampi, esāhaṁ bhante...*

Translation: Venerable Sir, I go for refuge to that Blessed One, though long passed away, as well as to his Teaching and the Order. May the Order graciously recognize me as a follower of the Buddha. For the second time, Venerable Sir ... For the third time, Venerable Sir ...

Taking refuge in the Triple Gem is effected by reciting the following passages, administered by the officiating monk:

Buddhaṁ saraṇaṁ gacchāmi. Dhammaṁ saraṇaṁ gacchāmi. Saṅghaṁ saraṇaṁ gacchāmi. Dutiyampi buddhaṁ ... Dutiyampi dhammaṁ ... Dutiyampi saṅghaṁ ... Tatiyampi buddhaṁ ... Tatiyampi dhammaṁ ... Tatiyampi saṅghaṁ ...

Translation: I go to the Buddha for refuge. I go to the Dharma for refuge. I go to the Order for refuge. For the second time … For the third time …

The confirmation ceremony is considered incomplete without the observance of the five precepts, although each serves a different purpose. The five precepts are thus dealt with in a separate lesson.

3

BEING A GOOD BUDDHIST

A Buddhist should not be satisfied with merely being a Buddhist; he should try to be a good Buddhist, too. Simply calling oneself a Buddhist without making an effort to live up to the name is not enough. Buddhism attaches more importance to actual practice than mere names. We should therefore learn what a good Buddhist is like and then try to be one.

1. A good Buddhist always holds the Buddha, the Dhamma, and the Saṅgha in

highest esteem. He does not act toward them, speak, or think of them in a disrespectful manner. Rejection of the Holy Triple Gem constitutes forfeiture of one's status as a Buddhist.

2. A good Buddhist not only has firm faith in the Three Gems, but tries also to understand the Buddha's teachings and Buddhist practices. He never ceases to acquire knowledge of the religion. He knows that sound knowledge in the religion will strengthen his faith and devotion.

3. A good Buddhist endeavors to apply the Buddha's teachings to his daily life. He makes religious practice part and parcel of his life and is ever conscious of its importance. He knows that a life without the Dharma is an incomplete and unsatisfactory one.

4. A good Buddhist loves and respects his (her) parents. He is obedient, courteous, and never argues back in an insolent manner. If, however, he wants to make his point clear, he takes care to do so in a respectful and polite manner. Furthermore, knowing that his parents love him dearly and sacrifice so much for him, he tries his best to return their love and, with a sense of filial gratitude, make himself useful to them and other family members. In short, a good Buddhist must also be a good son (or daughter); if he is not is a good son, then he cannot be a good Buddhist either.

5. A good Buddhist is a freethinker, he does not believe things just because they are told to him. He applies his own reasoning power and, if necessary, experiments

to find out the truth for himself.

6. A good Buddhist is broad-minded in matters like religious beliefs, traditions, and social values. He understands that people are different, and so are their beliefs, practices, and values. A good Buddhist knows what is best for him and always goes for the best.

7. A good Buddhist is honest, morally incorruptible and has strong will power. He knows that he must be responsible for all his actions and is therefore ever on his guard so that he may not do anything wrong. A good Buddhist takes delight in doing good and tries to avoid evil.

8. A good Buddhist is diligent, hard working, duty-conscious, and altruistic.

9. A good Buddhist, having studied and practiced the religion and being convinced of its teachings, tries his best to promote its spread and make it known to others. He knows that it is a great merit to share the Dharma with fellow beings.

4

BUDDHIST WORSHIP

Worship is usually understood as being expressions of reverence shown to deities or supernatural beings, who the worshippers believe are capable of preventing misfortunes and dangers, or granting them boons and blessings.

Every religion has a system of worship. In some religions worship can be very elaborate, time-consuming, and confusing. Others have simpler forms of worship. Some religions consider worship the central part of religious practice, while others assign it a secondary role. Thus, although worship exists in all religions, it is not the same, nor is it equally important.

Worship in Buddhism has a different meaning from other religions. It is the expression of love and respect for the Triple Gem, namely, the Buddha, the Dhamma, and the Saṅgha, rather than in so-called deities or supernatural beings. When we perform an act of worship, we do not do so in order to have the Triple Gem grant us anything, but in order to further strengthen our faith and inspiration to do good and to perfect ourselves. We know that the Buddha is the paragon of perfection, and worshipping him inculcates in us the wholesome aspiration to follow his teaching. We also know that all blessings in life come from our own good deeds. If we want those blessings, we must do good and conduct ourselves in a proper manner according to the Buddha's teaching.

When we worship, we should therefore concentrate on the virtues of the Buddha, the Dharma and the Saṅgha, not allowing our minds to be clouded with other thoughts or worries. We should feel our faith and conviction in the Three Gems grow in our hearts, and our determination to do good strengthened with every word of worship we utter.

Things to be borne in mind while worshipping:

1. You should not talk with friends or anybody close by. A good atmosphere of calm and quiet should be maintained. Do not disturb others with gossip.
2. You should not laugh or make jokes. To do so is considered a great disrespect.
3. You should never do such things as eating, drinking, smoking, or chewing gum.
4. You should sit (or stand) very still, make the body straight and firm. Do not shake your body, your head, hands or feet. You should not look around, but should pay full attention to the worship.

Recitation:

1. *Arahaṁ sammāsambuddho bhagavā.*
   Buddhaṁ bhagavantaṁ abhivādemi.
2. *Svākkhāto bhagavatā dhammo*
   dhammaṁ namassāmi.
3. *Supaṭipanno bhagavato sāvakasaṅgho*
   saṅghaṁ namāmi. (Bow down at the end of each.)

Translation: The Exalted One, far from defilements, perfectly self-enlightened: I bow low before the Buddha, the Exalted One.

The Dharma well expounded by the Blessed One: I bow low before the Dharma.

The Order of the Blessed One's disciple's of good conduct: I bow low before the Saṅgha.

Sitting posture

Thai Buddhists have a special way of sitting and prostrating. Please study the illustrations below:

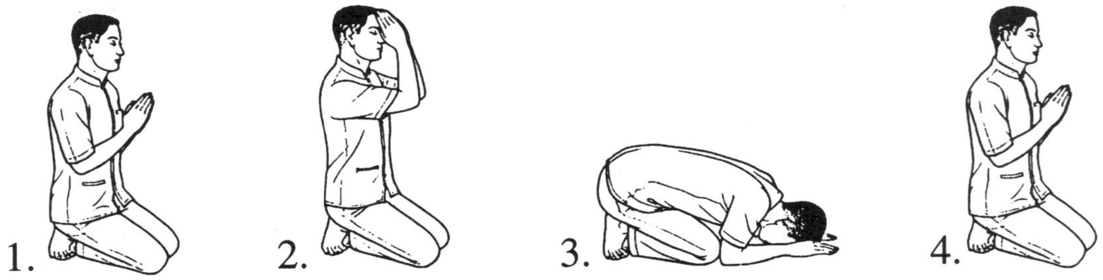

1. *Hands at chest level.*
2. *Lift hands to forehead.*
3. *Forehead, hands, elbows touch the ground.*
4. *Back to first position*
   (Women sit in the same way as men, but with the insteps flat on the floor.)

5
RECOLLECTION ON THE TRIPLE GEM

Buddhānussati

The Buddha was a great teacher who gave the world a religion unequaled in man's history. He was the embodiment of all virtues and this made him an object of supreme veneration for man and gods.

When we worship the Buddha, we pay homage to the Supreme Teacher; we meditate on his virtues and greatness and at the same time strengthen our faith and confidence in him. With a sense of gratitude and deference we renew our resolve to follow in his footsteps to enlighten ourselves and to render selfless service to others.

The following passage is recited as a means of concentration meditation practice. This kind of practice is called Buddhā-nussati or "Recollection on the Buddha." While reciting this we should, therefore, concentrate on the text and its meaning.

Pali

Itipi so bhagavā, arahaṁ, sammā sambuddho, vijjācaraṇa sampanno, sugato, lokavidū, anuttaro parisadammasārathi satthādeva-manussānaṁ, buddho, bhagavā'ti

Translation: Indeed he is the Blessed One, far from defilements, perfectly self-enlightened, fully possessed of wisdom and excellent conduct, one who has proceeded by the noble way, knower of the worlds, unexcelled trainer of trainable men, teacher of deities and men, the Awakened One, skillful in teaching Dharma.

Dhammānussati

Dhammānussati means Recollection of the Dharma. Even though the Buddha in his physical form is no more with us, we still have the Dharma as our guide and teacher. Thus the Dharma has virtually taken the place of the Buddha. In fact, the Dharma itself constitutes Buddhahood and Buddhahood is nothing but the realization of Dharma.

Buddhahood is achieved through the realization of the Dharma and there could never have been a Buddha without the Dharma. That is why the Buddha said: "He who sees the Dharma sees me, and he who sees me sees the Dharma." Obviously, "me" here does not mean the Buddha in his physical form, but the state of Buddhahood or Buddha-nature, through which the Dharma is realized. Thus in the ultimate sense both the Buddha and the Dharma are one and the same.

Like *Buddhānussati, Dhammānussati* is also recited as a means of concentration meditation practice. The following is the passage used for recollection of the Dharma:

Pali

Svākkhāto bhagavatā dhammo, sandiṭṭhiko, akāliko, ehipassiko, opanayiko, paccattaṁ veditabbo viññūhī ti

Translation: Well-expounded is the Dharma by the Blessed One, to be realized by oneself, with immediate result, capable of standing the test, leading to Nirvana, to be attained by the wise, each for himself.

It is clear from the above passage that the Dharma is something to be practiced, not merely studied or memorized. To practice Dharma means to follow the teachings of the Buddha and to come closer to Buddha-nature. Remember that the Dharma will benefit us only when we seriously practice it.

Saṅghānussati

The third of the Three Gems, the Noble Saṅgha, came into existence the moment Koṇḍañña attained the Eye of Truth. Since then the number of the Buddha's noble disciples continued to grow at a phenomenal rate and they all helped the Master in one way or another to spread the Dharma.

The Buddha discovered the Dharma and taught it to the world, but without the

Saṅgha his teachings would not spread very far or last much longer after he passed away, and the world today would have no chance to benefit from them.

The noble disciples, having realized the Dharma, work to enlighten others. The Order of Monks, too, studies, practices and teaches the Dharma. They are the treasurers and the protectors of the Dharma. This is how the tradition continues. The Saṅgha therefore plays a significant role in the preservation and spread of the religion. The fact that we still have relatively easy access to the Buddha's teachings today, over 2,500 years after the Great Demise, is due largely to the efforts and sacrifice of the Saṅgha.

Saṅghānussati means Recollection of the Saṅgha. The Pali passage is as follows:

Pali

Supaṭipanno bhagavato sāvakasaṅgho
ujupaṭipanno bhagavato sāvakasaṅgho
ñāyapaṭipanno bhagavato sāvakasaṅgho
sāmīcipaṭipanno bhagavato sāvakasaṅgho
yadidaṁ cattāri purisayugāni aṭṭhapurisapuggalā
esa bhagavato sāvakasaṅgho
āhuneyyo, pāhuneyyo, dakkhiṇeyyo, añjalīkaraṇīyo
anuttaraṁ puññakkhettaṁ lokassā ti

Translation: The Order of the Blessed One's disciples is of good conduct: the Order of the Blessed One's disciples is of upright conduct; the Order of the Blessed One's disciples is of dutiful conduct; the Order of the Blessed One's disciples is of proper conduct. This Order, namely, the four pairs of men, the eight individuals, that is the Order of the Blessed One's disciples, worthy of gifts, worthy of hospitality, worthy of offerings, worthy of reverential salutation, an incomparable field of merits to the world.

The phrases "four pairs of men" and "eight kinds of individuals" refer to those people, men and women, who have attained one of the four levels of enlightenment, called Stream Entry, Once Returner, Non-Returner or Arahatship, which is full enlightenment.

6

THE FIVE PRECEPTS

The Pali term for the five precepts is *"pañcasīla."* The five precepts are the basic moral codes of conduct that every lay Buddhist should follow.

A person can take the precepts by making a resolution with himself, but it is customary to have them administered by a monk or, where one is not available, by a novice.

When we want to take the five precepts from a monk, we first recite, with palms together, the request passage which runs as follows:

Mayaṁ bhante, visuṁ visuṁ rakkhanatthāya, tisaraṇena saha, pañcasīlāni yācāma. Dutiyampi, mayaṁ ... Tatiyampi, mayaṁ ...

(Venerable Sir, we seek from you, for individual observance, the five precepts along with the Three Gems. For the second time ... For the third time ...)

The monk would then recite three times the Preliminary Homage and the devotees repeat after him:

Namo tassa bhagavato arahato sammāsambuddhassa.

(Homage to Him, the Blessed One, the Exalted One, the Fully-Enlightened One.)

Then follows the acceptance of the Three Gems as our refuge, to be repeated sentence by sentence after the monk.

Buddhaṁ saraṇaṁ gacchāmi.

Dhammaṁ saraṇaṁ gacchāmi.

Saṅghaṁ saraṇaṁ gacchāmi.

Dutiyampi buddhaṁ ...

Tatiyampi buddhaṁ ...

(I go to the Buddha for refuge. I go to the Dharma for refuge. I go to the Saṅgha for refuge. For the second time ... For the third time ...)

Then the monk concludes: *Tisaraṇa-gamanaṁ niṭṭhitaṁ.* (The Going for the Three Refuges is now complete) and we respond with: *Āma bhante* (So it is, Venerable Sir). This summing up can be left out, but it should be learned as many monks do include it in the procedure.

Now the monk recites the five precepts one by one to be repeated by the lay devotee

(1) Pāṇātipātā veramaṇī sikkhāpadaṁ samādiyāmi.

(2) Adinnādānā veramaṇī ...

(3) Kāmesu micchācārā veramaṇī ...

(4) Musāvādā veramaṇī ...

(5) Surā-merayamajja-pamādaṭṭhānā veramaṇī ...

(I observe the precept refraining from (1) killing; (2) stealing; (3) sexual misconduct; (4) falsehood; (5) intoxicants that cause carelessness)

Having completed the recitation of the five precepts, the monk then concludes as follows:

Imāni pañcasikkhāpadāni. Sīlena sugatiṁ yanti sīlena bhogasampadā sīlena nibbutiṁ

yanti tasmā sīlaṁ visodhaye.

(These, then, are the five precepts. *Sīla* leads to a happy state, *sīla* leads to prosperity, *sīla* leads to peace. Therefore, keep *sīla* ever pure.)

The devotees respond with: *Sādhu*! (It is well.) Then they prostrate three times. The procedure is now complete.

It is clear from the wording of the text that these precepts are not commandments, but moral codes that we willingly undertake to observe out of clear understanding and firm conviction that they are good for ourselves and our society. Our life would be a truly happy one and our society would become a much safer and more peaceful place to live in if these precepts were observed in earnest. When we examine the social implications of the five precepts, we find that:

The first precept implies the rights to life of all living beings. It also implies the importance of love and compassion for all.

The second precept signifies a person's rights for the possession as well as the protection of wealth rightly acquired. It also stresses the importance of right livelihood.

The third precept, not to indulge in sexual misconduct, teaches one to respect one's own spouse as well as those of others, including, by extension, all things that are near and dear to them. It is, moreover, intended to inculcate self-restraint and a sense of social propriety.

The fourth precept aims at preserving our credibility, upon which rests our honor, dignity, and trustworthiness. It makes us honest and truthful.

The last precept is intended to keep us healthy physically, mentally, and morally. It helps us to maintain our sense of responsibility in thought and action—something not possible when we are under the spell of drink or drugs.

We can see, therefore, that the five precepts are not only good, but absolutely necessary for a truly happy and peaceful society.

7

THAILAND AND BUDDHISM

Thailand is a beautiful and thriving country in Southeast Asia. It has an area of 198,455 square miles—some 50,000 square miles larger than Japan. Its present population is 55 million, 93 percent of whom are Buddhist.

Buddhism has had a deep influence on the Thai nation as a whole. It has molded the life of the people, their thoughts and behavior. Its influence can be seen in all spheres of life and activities, in architecture, painting and sculpture, in manners and speech, in language, traditions and forms of entertainment, rites and ceremonies, and in all other forms of Thai culture.

The written history of Thailand dates back some 800 years, long after the Thai nation actually came into existence. Recent archaeological finds in various parts of the country have produced evidence that civilization in the area can be traced back as far as 6,000 years ago. It is still uncertain, however, as to what race actually did occupy the region.

The word "Thai" means "free." Thailand is thus the "Land of the Free." Thai people take great pride in this name because during the 800 years of her history the country as a whole never lost her independence or freedom. Even when Western colonialism in S. E. Asia was at its peak and the countries around her fell one after another under Western rule, Thailand was able to preserve her sovereignty.

According to the Mahāvaṁsa, the Great Chronicle of Sri Lanka, Buddhism came to the area that is now Thailand more than 2,000 years ago, during the reign of Emperor Asoka of India. Since the day of its arrival until the present the religion has occupied an undisputed position as the most popular faith of the people. Today Thailand is the only country in the world that has institutionalized Buddhism as the state religion.

Since ancient times, Thai rulers have been Buddhist and great patrons of the religion. They encouraged and supported Buddhism by building and maintaining monasteries, casting new Buddha images and restoring old ones, providing monks with material necessities and assisting them in their religious duties. Many Thai kings and princes entered the Order, either for life or for limited periods of time, in order to devote more time to the study and practice of the religion. Some of them, like King Li Thai and King Mongkut, even became great scholars in Buddhism and the Pali language. Since 1903 the State has passed laws, called Saṅgha Acts, to give the Order more power for its internal administration.

The Department of Religious Affairs has been established in the Ministry of Education in order to provide an effective channel of communication and cooperation between the Saṅgha and the State. In addition to Buddhism, the department is also responsible for the affairs of all other religions in the country.

There are two main sects of Buddhism, Theravada and Mahayana. Theravada means "Teaching of the Elders" and Mahayana means "The Great Vehicle." Thai Buddhism belongs to the former. Here the institution of monks, the Saṅgha, plays an important role in religious affairs and activities. According to tradition, every young man in Thailand is expected, though not compelled, to enter the Order, at least for a brief period, in order to acquaint himself with the religion. The number of monks in the country is, therefore, considerably large—about 300,000 at any given time.

Thai monks shave their hair and eyebrows every month (on the full moon eve); they wear brownish yellow robes (color shades may vary); they do not take solid food after midday until the following dawn; they refrain from physical contact with women and from all forms of sexual activity. Altogether there are 227 rules in the *Pāṭimokkha* (the main body of the monks' discipline) that regulate their conduct.

Buddhist monks devote their time to studying scriptures and other subjects, meditation, teaching, helping people with their problems, giving advice when needed, and doing social work. They work for the benefit and well-being of society without expecting remuneration or rewards in any form and are supported in their work by lay devotees. The Buddhist principle underlying social service is universal love and altruism, which is amply exemplified in the monks' conduct and activities.

8

BUDDHIST HOLY DAYS

There are five major Buddhist holy days celebrated in Thailand. They are Māgha Pūjā, Visākha Pūjā, Āsāḷha Pūjā, Lent Commencement Day, and Lent Ending Day. We Buddhists should know the origin and significance of these important days. Some of the days are celebrated with equal zeal by other Buddhist countries, while others are treated with less enthusiasm.

Māgha Pūjā Day

Māgha Pūjā Day falls on the full moon of the third lunar month, somewhere toward the end of February. *"Māgha,"* like Visākha and Āsāḷha, is the name of a month in the lunar calendar used in ancient India. The word *"pūjā"* signifies worship. So Māgha Pūjā means the worship in the month of Māgha.

Māgha Pūjā Day is also known as the day of the Fourfold Assembly. This was a special assembly that took place at the Bamboo Grove (Veḷuvana) and contained four extraordinary features, namely:

1. It was the full moon day of the month Māgha.
2. 1,250 monk disciples assembled to see the Buddha, all of their own accord, without an appointment.
3. All these monks were Arahants who had attained the sixfold super knowledge.
4. All of them were the Buddha's direct disciples, having been ordained by the Lord himself.

At the fourfold assembly the Buddha gave the monks an important discourse summarizing his teachings into three main principles, namely, (1) not to do any evil; (2) to do good; and (3) to purify the mind. These three principles are fundamental in the Buddhist doctrine.

Māgha Pūjā Day is also known as the Dharma Day as it was the occasion on which an important Dharma discourse was delivered by the Buddha.

Māgha Pūjā Day is important in another respect. It is said that in the last year of his life, just three months before his passing away, the Buddha had determined the day he would die and announced it to his disciples. The incident is known as the Rejection of the Aggregates of Life and it also took place on the full moon of the third lunar month (Māgha). This fact adds more significance to the Māgha Pūjā Day and makes it even more sacred for Buddhists.

On Māgha Pūjā Day, faithful Buddhists will go to the temple in the morning. They observe the five precepts, listen to a sermon, serve food for monks, meditate or take part in other forms of meritorious activities. They also perform circumambulation, walking around a shrine or a Buddha image three times, as a gesture of faith and respect in the Triple Gem.

Visākha Puja day

This is the most sacred occasion for the whole Buddhist world. It marks the three important events in the Buddha's life: his birth, enlightenment, and the Great Demise, which all took place on the full moon of the sixth lunar month (Visākha).

The Buddha was born in 623 B.C. Seven days after Siddhattha's birth, his mother, Queen Māyā, died and the baby prince was thereafter looked after by his foster mother, Pajāpatī. He was an extraordinary person, extremely intelligent and compassionate, and it was predicted that he would one day become either a Universal Monarch or a Buddha

Despite all the comfort and luxury of a royal household, Prince Siddhattha decided at the age of twenty-nine to leave home and family and become a wandering monk in search of the Truth. He labored hard for six long years, experimenting with all kinds of spiritual practices and meditation. Then, on the full moon of the month Visākha, at exactly thirty-five years of age, he attained enlightenment and became the Buddha, the Enlightened One.

The Buddha worked hard for forty-five years to spread his teachings and to enlighten people and so established the religion now known as Buddhism.

The Buddha passed away at the age of eighty, again on the full moon day of Visākha, leaving behind an invaluable legacy, a spiritual heritage that has served the world through a long and far-reaching dissemination of over 2,500 years.

In Thailand Visākha Pūjā is celebrated in very much the same way as Māgha, except on a larger scale and with more enthusiasm. In Sri Lanka, to the south of India, it is the year's biggest and most festive event. Visākha is, in fact, celebrated in all Buddhist countries and by all Buddhist communities. The day is also known as the Buddha Day as it commemorates the three important events in the Buddha's life.

Āsāḷha Puja Day

The Buddha attained enlightenment at Buddha-Gaya (Bodh-Gaya) on the full moon of Visākha. Two months later at the Deer Park near Benares he delivered the first discourse to his first five disciples, Koṇḍañña, Vappa, Bhaddiya, Mahānāma, and Assaji. This epoch-making incident marked the establishment of the Buddhist religion.

It was on the full moon of Āsāḷha, the eighth lunar month, that the first discourse was delivered. At the end of the sermon Koṇḍañña attained the Eye of Truth; the Order of Saṅgha was initiated and the Triple Gem became complete. There are thus three reasons why Āsāḷha Pūjā Day is celebrated by Buddhists:

1. On that day the Buddha delivered the first discourse;
2. The religion was established;
3. The Saṅgha came into existence and the Triple Gem became complete. (For this reason it is also known as Saṅgha Day.)

The name of the first discourse is Dhammacakkappavattana Sutta. "*Dhammacakka*" means the Wheel of Dharma and the whole word means "Setting into Motion the Wheel of Dharma." "*Sutta*" means a discourse. The main theme of the first sermon is the Four Noble Truths: suffering (*dukkha*), the cause of suffering, the end of suffering, and the way to the end of suffering. These Truths are universal and invariably valid at all times and in all places. That is why they are called Noble Truths.

The first Truth states that existence is unsatisfactory, incomplete, empty, subject to change and undesirable. Because of this we have to suffer one way or another. For example, we cannot be happy all the time even if we want to; we are born, grow old, become weak, and die; we are separated from those we love and care for. All these and other undesirable elements are the normal conditions in life.

The second Truth explains the cause of suffering. Everything that exists comes under the law of cause and effect. This law operates in all spheres, and at all levels of existence. Suffering can be removed, according to this law, by destroying its causes.

The third and the fourth Truths show the way out of suffering. Nirvana is the end of suffering (third truth). It is the state of perfect calm and bliss, the ultimate freedom from all forms of suffering. One can reach this state by following the Eightfold Path, also known as the Middle Way (fourth Truth), which comprises Right Understanding, Right Thought, Right Speech, Right Action, Right Livelihood, Right Effort, Right Mindfulness, and Right Concentration. This is the way to true happiness.

The Rains Retreat

The day following the Āsāḷha full moon is called the Lent Commencement Day or *Vassupanayika* in Pali. The Lent, or Rains Residence (Retreat), is one of the monastic observances originated in the time of the Lord Buddha.

When Buddhism was first established the number of monks was relatively small and the Saṅgha organization was more manageable. Monks did not stay at any particular place, but were mostly on the move in their mission to spread the Buddha's teachings. During the rainy season, when the country experienced heavy and frequent rainfall, it was difficult for them to travel around. The season was also the time for farmers to cultivate their land and grow crops. It was, naturally, the time for most ascetics to stop wandering and remain stationed in a specific place.

The Buddha therefore established a rule by which monks are obliged to remain posted at a certain place, preferably a monastery, for a period of three months, starting from the first day of the eighth waning moon (i.e., the day following the Āsāḷha full-moon).

During these three months, monks cannot spend the night outside the area they have taken for rains residence. If they have to go out, they must return before the dawn of the following day. There are exceptions to this rule by which a monk is allowed to spend the night elsewhere; for instance, when one of his parent is seriously ill, or he is required for some urgent religious work at a place too far away to return in one day, but even in such cases, he may be away only for seven days at a stretch. This practice, like many others, is preserved to the letter down to this day and the period is considered by all Buddhists as exceptionally sacred for performing merits, or taking vows for spiritual development.

In some Buddhist countries this is a favored time for young men to enter the monkhood and stay in a monastery in order to acquaint themselves better with the religion—something they cannot conveniently do while leading a household life. The number of monks during the Lent in such countries is therefore much greater than at any other time of the year. This is particularly true of Thailand, where the Buddhist tradition is still very much alive and strong.

Religious activities usually increase for both monks and the laity during the Rains Retreat. Monasteries conduct special courses for new Saṅgha members and intensive meditation classes and Dharma lectures may also be organized for both parties.

In Thailand it is during the Lent, especially, that the Great Birth discourses are delivered, often with great pomp and show. This is the story of King Vessantara, the Bodhisatta who took birth in order to fulfill the Perfection of Giving (*dāna paramita*). The story has exerted a deep influence on the Thai national character as a whole and helps to explain, at least partly, why Thai people are so noted for their kindheartedness and generosity.

As the Lent is regarded a sacred period, it has become a common practice among the more devout Buddhists to make a vow to abstain from undesirable habits that they want to get rid of, or to commit themselves to certain practices for their spiritual progress. For instance, they may resolve to give up alcoholic drinks or cigarettes, or take a vow to practice meditation for a certain length of time on a daily basis, or observe the five precepts more strictly. In short, they perform merits in any way possible, and try to learn and practice the Dhamma with greater determination and effort, partly as a means to perfect themselves and partly as a practical tribute (*paṭipattipūjā*) to the Lord Buddha.

At the end of three months, i.e., on the full moon of the eleventh lunar month (usually mid-October), Buddhists hold a ceremony to mark the termination of the Lent. This is Lent Ending Day, also known as *Pavāraṇā* Day. Lay devotees go to the temple in large numbers and share food with monks in the traditional way called *piṇḍapāta*.

First the lay devotees, with bowls of rice, curries, and other offerings, line up at an appointed place. When all is in order, a signal is given to inform the monks in the monastery who then form a single or double file, according to seniority of ordination. With eyes cast down and food-bowls in hands, they walk slowly along the lines of devotees receiving their offerings with composure and grace. Thus they continue until the last devotee has had the opportunity to serve them his food. Then they all assemble in the main hall, where the lay followers perform other kinds of meritorious activities, such as determining the five or eight precepts, listening to a sermon, and meditating. Various cultural programs may also be staged to entertain and educate the people.

The practice of alms round mentioned above has its origin in a story allegedly connected with the Buddha. According to this, the Buddha once went to spend the Rains Retreat in Tāvatiṁsa Heaven, where he delivered the Abhidhamma teachings to Māyādevaputta (his mother Māyā in her previous life) and other gods. At the end of the Lent, he returned to earth to great rejoicing and celebration. This was in the seventh year after the enlightenment. Accordingly, ceremonies and festivities are held in order to commemorate the event.

The Kaṭhina Ceremony

Kaṭhina" in Pali refers to the wooden frame upon which monks in ancient India used to sew their robes. The robes thus prepared came to be known as Kaṭhina robes. The Buddha allowed Kaṭhina robes to be presented to the monks who have completed the three-month period of Rains Retreat. The event in which the robes

are offered to the monks is, therefore, known as the Kaṭhina Ceremony or, more popularly, the Robe-Presentation Ceremony.

There are several reasons why the Kaṭhina has come to occupy so much importance in Buddhist monasticism and among the Buddhist public:

1. It can be done only once a year for each monastery and it must take place within a specific period of time, never before or after. (See below.)

2. The ceremony enables participating monks to extend the benefit period, in which monks are allowed certain minor privileges, from one month (from the day following the Lent Ending Day) to four extra months right through the cold season.

3. Traditionally, Buddhists believe that offerings made to individual monks accrue less merit than those made in the name of the Saṅgha (a group of four monks or more). The Kaṭhina robes can be presented only to the Saṅgha; at least five monks must be present in order for this ceremony to be fulfilled.

4. The Lent is a period during which religious activities in the monasteries are at their peak: there are more monks, more intensive spiritual training, and more social service activities. Offerings made to monks engaged in such meritorious work are believed to acquire much merit and ensure great happiness and prosperity in life.

The story of the origination of the Kaṭhina ceremony concerns a group of thirty monks from Patha township who went to Sāvatthī to see the Buddha, who was then residing at Jeta Grove (Jetavana). They could make it only to Saketa, a neighboring town of Sāvatthī, when the day to observe the Rains arrived, and they were compelled to break off their journey and stay there for the three rainy months. They were disappointed at not being able to see the Buddha as planned.

When the Rains ended, they hastened to Sāvatthī. There they sought audience with the Master, who, perceiving a need for extra robes for monks after the rains retreat, decreed a provision for monks to accept the robes given by devotees within the one-month period from the first day of the eleventh waning moon to the full moon of the twelfth lunar month (i.e., between mid-October and mid-November).

Since then, it has become a tradition for Buddhist devotees to help in the fulfillment of this special provision. Monks who have not completed the Rains are, however, excluded from this privilege.

In Thailand, the Kaṭhina ceremony is often accompanied by great festivities and colorful celebration. The robes and extra offerings, if any, are taken to the monastery for which they are intended, and to which the donors' intention has already been made known. They are then presented to the assembly of the Saṅgha in accordance with a prescribed formula and procedure.

When the statement of dedication has been duly pronounced by the lay followers, one of the Saṅgha members proceeds to make a formal announcement so the matter may become absolutely clear to the whole assembly. Another then makes a proposal as to who should represent the Saṅgha to receive and make use of the robes. Normally, the name of the abbot or a very senior monk in the monastery is quoted and then, if no objection is raised, approved by the Saṅgha.

Once the presentation ceremony is completed, it becomes the duty of the Saṅgha to reassemble in the *Uposatha* Hall and perform certain ecclesiastical rites dictated by the Discipline (*Vinaya*). An *Uposatha* Hall is a place for special rites performed by the Saṅgha. Such rites are exclusively for monks and no lay persons can take part in them.

Thai Buddhists often mix merit making with fun and foreigners are baffled by the obvious lack of solemnity in most Thai religious events. One should understand, however, that such functions are generally organized in two parts: the traditional, nonreligious, festive celebration and the solemn religious aspect. Of these two parts the first is, of course, more popular.

Songkran Day

Two New Year Days are celebrated by Thai people: one is the regular New Year Day, which falls on January 1, and the other is called the Songkran Day, which falls on April 13. Songkran is the traditional Thai New Year Day; it is an important occasion for merit making and a high time for fun and games.

There is an interesting Thai folk story connected with the Songkran Day. It tells how there once lived in a certain village an extraordinary boy by the name of Dhanapala. He was born into a very rich family, and was extremely intelligent and kindhearted. He even knew the languages of animals and could understand the humming of bees and the songs of birds. People had great respect for him and his fame spread far and wide until it finally reached the ears of a rather strange but powerful god. This was Kapila Brahma, the god with four faces, who could see in four directions all at once.

Kapila was a conceited god. He could not bear to think that there was anyone so intelligent and kind as to command the respect of so many people. He felt that people had begun to place more faith in Dhanapala than in himself. This he did not like and would not tolerate.

One day he came down from heaven and challenged Dhanapala to answer three questions: "Where is a person's 'glow' in the morning? Where is it at midday? Where is it in the evening?" The stakes were high: if the boy could answer the questions, Kapila would offer his own head to him; if he could not, then he would have to give his head to Kapila as a trophy for his triumph. Dhanapala accepted the challenge and promised to find the answers in seven days.

Six days passed by and Dhanapala could find no answers, but he was helped by some sympathetic deities, who transformed themselves into eagles and discussed the answer to the riddle within earshot of Dhanapala. By listening to their conversation, Dhanapala discovered the answers to Kapila's riddles.

The answer is that in the morning a person's glow is in the face, because people always wash their faces in the morning to greet the day. During the day, when the weather is hot, people bathe themselves, splashing water over the chest, so at midday the glow is in the chest. In the evening, coming home from work, they wash their feet before going up in to the house. Thus in the evening the glow is in the feet. In a more abstract but meaningful interpretation, in the morning we must put on a cheerful face, beginning the day on the right foot; during the day we must wear a brave heart to deal with the business of the day; in the evening when we come home from work we must be able to "wash our feet," that is, let go of the day's activities and greet our family with a cheerful demeanor.

Kapila lost the bet and was therefore compelled to cut off his head according to their agreement. Before fulfilling his promise, however, the unfortunate Brahma proclaimed:

"I am a very powerful god. If my head is dropped on the ground, the whole world will burst into flames. If my head is thrown into the ocean, the ocean will dry up immediately. And if it is thrown up into the air, there will be no rain for seven years!"

To avoid this catastrophe, the god Kapila ordered his seven daughters to take turns carrying his head in a big golden bowl, each for a period of one year. So the Songkran Day marks the occasion when Kapila's head changes hands—and the year changes too!

There is an important message hidden in this unusual story. The four faces of

Brahma symbolize the four Sublime Virtues taught by the Buddha, namely, Loving-kindness (*mettā*), Compassion (*karuṇā*), Sympathetic Joy (*muditā*), and Impartiality or Equanimity (*upekkhā*). These four virtues are the qualities of the mind essential for peaceful coexistence and cooperation in society. If people do not practice them, but throw them away, there is great trouble in society. So these four virtues should be carried along, i.e., practiced, as carefully as the Brahma's head was carried.

On Songkran Day, Buddhists go to the temple to make merit. They worship the Buddha, offer food to monks, observe the five precepts, bathe the Buddha image, and meditate. Young people take delight in splashing water at each other (hence the name "Water Splashing Festival"); they sing together, play games and generally have fun. Friends laugh and enjoy themselves, enemies become friends and forget their past conflicts. Songkran is, indeed, an occasion to cultivate good qualities or virtues in our hearts

8

WESTERN BUDDHISM AT A GLANCE

Professor Rhys Davids, a Buddhist scholar of international standing, speaks of his deep conviction in Buddhism:

"I have examined every one of the great religions of the world, and in none of them have I found anything to surpass the beauty and comprehensiveness of the Four Noble Truths of the Buddha. I am content to shape my life according to that path."

The Four Noble Truths referred to by this intellectual giant constitute the core of Buddhism, which has become increasingly popular in the Western world and is gaining ground in all levels of society, especially among intellectuals.

The history of the religion in the West begins at a very early period. Originated in India some 600 years before the birth of Christ, Buddhism made its first contact with the West in the fourth century B.C. when Alexander the Great (356-323 B.C.) invaded India in a series of ambitious war missions to conquer the East. He was deeply appreciative of arts and sciences, having in his army a considerable number of scholars, experts, and artists in various fields. They consequently took the opportunity to acquaint themselves with the cultural elements of India, including those of Buddhism, which was by then widespread. Alexander's conquest of India was brief and his rule in the country short-lived, but the consequences of both were far-reaching.

An end to the Greek occupation of India was ushered in by Emperor Chandragupta (321?c. – 296 B.C.), who established the Maurya dynasty and was identified with Sandrocottus in the Greek accounts. His reign witnessed the establishment of diplomatic relations between the Greek rulers and India.

The Maurya dynasty found the greatest son in Emperor Asoka, who succeeded his father Bindusara to the throne in the year 218 of the Buddhist Era (B.E.). His was a rich and extensive empire: on the northwest it included the states of Paropanisadae (Kabul), Aria (Herat), Arachosia (Kandahar), and parts of Gedrosia (Baluchistan), yielded to Chandragupta by Seleucus I Nicator; on the northeast it stretched as far as Kamarupa (Assam), and included Kashmir and Nepal; southward it extended to cover most of the Indian peninsula as far as the Penner River. A great deal of information about Asoka and his reign comes from the numerous stone inscriptions and the many religious edifices he left throughout the empire. He was not a born Buddhist, but a converted one. Once a Buddhist, however, he went to great length, with a zeal and enthusiasm unequaled in the history of the religion, to propagate the Buddha's doctrines. It is also during his reign that India's diplomatic relations with the Western world were at their height. He was, indeed, the moving force behind the earliest dissemination of the Buddhist doctrines to the West, and the diplomatic intercourse provided a wholesome channel through which he successfully implemented the noble schemes of the "Missions of Piety."

In three of his Edicts (Rock Edicts II, V and XIII), Asoka described how he had, in the thirteenth year after his coronation, instituted five-yearly circuits of officials whose charge was to proclaim the moral law, and in the following year he instituted the *Dharma-mahamatras*, an equivalent of the Ministry of Religious Affairs. The Edicts also speak of the "Mission of Piety" he sent to many countries, including five Greek territories whose kings have been identified as Antiochus II of Syria (261-246 B.C.), Antigonas Gonatas of Macedonia (276-246 B.C.), Ptolemy II of Egypt (285-247 B.C.), Alexander of Epirus (272-258 B.C.), and Magas of Cyrene (300-258 B.C.).

That Buddhism was known to the ancient Greeks and even practiced by them there can be no reasonable doubt. Since the second century B.C. down to the days of Christ, Buddhism was an active force in the regions where Christ grew up and preached. The influences of Buddhism on early Christianity cannot be ruled out. (Christian monasticism, for example, seems to have been influenced by that of Buddhism, which was the first religion in history to establish and organize cenobitic monasticism.) An Asoka Edict recently discovered in Afghanistan, once part of the Asoka empire, bears inscriptions in both the Greek and Aramaic languages, the latter being the language of Christ. The ancient Greeks are known to have developed some very advanced and sophisticated philosophical systems, which the Christians later incorporated to enrich their religion. It is not as yet definite how far Buddhist thought was known to those Greek philosophers, but the possibility cannot be dismissed altogether. For such hypothetical conclusions, however, students of religious history should exercise their judgment with care and discretion.

The Greeks who settled in India were, no doubt, greatly influenced by Buddhism and their number might have been considerable. They were, in fact, the first to create Buddha images. The discovery of many Asoka edicts in the Greek language, whose contents are largely identical with their Indian counterparts, indicates that they were made solely for Greek-speaking communities in the country.

Mahāvaṁsa, the Chronicle of Sri Lanka (Ceylon), compiled in the fifth century but based on much earlier materials, narrates how in the first century B.C. a group of Buddhist monks from the Greek City of Alexandria (Yonanagara-Alasanda) attended the inauguration ceremony of the Great Stupa Ratanamali at Anuradhapura in Sri Lanka. The delegation was headed by a Greek monk named Dhammarakkhita the Great. This clearly shows that Buddhism was then a flourishing religion in Greek territories.

Further evidence to the point under discussion is found in *The Questions of Milinda* (*Milindapañhā*), a Buddhist classic written in the Pali language around the first century. This treatise records a lengthy debate between King Milinda and the Elder Nāgasena. The former has been identified with the Greek king, Menandros, whose rule over the northwestern part of India dates back to the first century B.C. He is said to be one of the most well-versed in the Buddhist doctrine, and was able to expound it with great eloquence. One of the most oft-quoted Buddhist texts, this literary masterpiece contributed in no small measure to the early exposition of the Buddha's teachings.

References such as those quoted clearly testify to the early prevalence of Buddhism in certain regions in the West since ancient time and its impact on early Christianity. But the scarcity of literary evidence in the West makes it difficult to pinpoint the nature and the extent of the Buddhist role here. One cannot help wondering if this scarcity of "evidence" is the result of a wholesale destruction caused by narrow-minded religious fanatics in later periods, who were antagonistic to Buddhism. Whether this is the case is a subject for the students of religious history to investigate. Nevertheless, it is well known that the religious fervor and fanaticism of the early Christians were responsible for much bloodshed and violence against the so-called "heretics" who did not agree with traditional Christianity. Early Christian irrational hostility to freedom of thought and the advancement of science is a matter of historical record.

After a lapse of many centuries when the link of the past was long disconnected, Buddhism once again began to make itself felt on the Western horizon. This time the religion was welcomed with much zeal and enthusiasm and the prospect seemed more encouraging. Although the Westerners' interest in the religion was primarily academic, yet the very appeal of its sublime teachings did command their respect and admiration and has succeeded in winning a number of the more knowledgeable to the faith. The very fact that the religion had, in the first place, gained the attention of academicians and free thinkers works out well for its creditability and, hence, its acceptability. Centers for Buddhist studies and practices were inaugurated in universities and colleges; various organizations devoted to religio-social activities as well as to the dissemination of the faith came into being. The influx in recent years of Indo-Chinese refugees, who are by and large Buddhist, provides a new impetus and has spurred the growth to dramatic proportions.

Of the Theravada countries, Sri Lanka, though somewhat limited in resources and manpower, seems to be in the forefront in missionary activities in the West. The Mahā Bodhi Society, with its headquarters in Sri Lanka and branch offices all over the world, is one of the most successful pioneers in the field. Sri Lankan monks are active in organizing community activities, meditation retreats, or coordinating with other groups in social service endeavors. A few of them are engaged in teaching Buddhism in colleges and universities. The Burmese have also made valuable contributions mostly in the field of meditation and Abhidhamma studies in which they are known to specialize.

Thailand became involved in international missionary activities in comparatively recent time, but its role and potential cannot be underestimated. The Thais have opened up, during the past two or three decades, quite a few temples around the world. Now there are some forty Thai temples in the United States, all active and determined in their efforts to propagate the Buddha's teachings; there are, in addition, many more lay organizations dedicated to the spread of the religion. Thai- or Burmese-trained Westerners, some of whom are monks, try to make the knowledge of Buddhism available to as many interested individuals as possible. According to statistics published in 1969, there were 254 Buddhist groups, centers, societies, temples and missions in the United States, 84 in Hawaii alone. The increase in number of those organizations and their activities in the last two decades is very impressive.

Laotians and Cambodians are other major groups in the United States and some European countries. They are also large in number and have contributed in no small measure to the growth of Buddhism in this part of the world.

Among the Mahayana countries, Japan is one of the most active in the Western scene. With a century's experience, Japanese Buddhists in the West today are one of the best organized. The Tibetans are another important group; their presence became more conspicuous here since the annexation of their country to China around the middle of the century. Both Japan and Tibet are highly successful; they have established centers of learning, colleges, and universities all over the United States and their religious organizations keep expanding by leaps and bounds. The success of the Chinese, Koreans, and Vietnamese is also impressive. (The Chinese are, in fact, among the earliest arrivals.) They have a nationwide network in the United

States and a host of affiliated organizations. Their membership is considerable and their contribution significant.

The greatest contribution to the growth of Buddhism in the West in the field of academic research and studies comes, however, from the Westerners themselves. Not all of these scholars are Buddhist, but their appreciation and respect for the Buddha's teachings is genuine. The first impetus for serious studies of the religion in its multifarious aspects may be said to be generated in the early nineteenth century by no less a person than the German philosopher Schopenhauer (1788 – 1860), who aroused an interest among Western thinkers and intellectuals through his references to Buddhist philosophy. A systematic and scientific study of Buddhism was undertaken by Eugene Burnouf (1801 – 1852), the French orientalist. His *Essai sur le Pali* saw the daylight in 1926 and the years that followed its publication witnessed a series of attempts to produce even greater works and to expand the fields of research. Everywhere in Europe—Belgium, the Netherlands, France, Switzerland, Germany, Italy, England—Buddhist temples, associations, and study centers began to mushroom. Australia is certainly not trailing behind Europe and America; Thai, Sri Lankan, and other temples have already been founded and are well organized and attended. The beginning there was typically a modest one, but current developments are quite promising.

England must be mentioned, above all, as having rendered the greatest service to Buddhism in the West. Here the name of T.W. Rhys Davids, whom we quoted at the beginning of this chapter, should be singled out as one of the most, if not the most, outstanding champions for the Buddhist cause. He founded, in 1881, the Pali Text Society with an aim "to render accessible to students the rich stores of the earliest Buddhist literature." The service this society has contributed toward the dissemination of the knowledge of Buddhism in the West is still unsurpassed. It has succeeded in bringing out in Roman characters all the Pali texts of the Buddhist scriptures. Their English translations, numbering some fifty-eight volumes, and many treatises by authorities from both the East and the West have also been published. In addition, the society has edited Pali Commentaries of the Tripitaka, numbering some sixty volumes, as well as a number of post-canonical works.

Thanks to the efforts and sacrifice of all these scholars, many in the West have now come to understand and respect the religion as one abounding in wisdom and profound philosophy. William Macquitty, a renowned scholar, observes: "With the advance of science and psychology many of the older faiths have suffered. Their beliefs went against the new knowledge and the new knowledge won. But in this conflict the teaching of Buddha required no adjustments. Its wisdom has encompassed everything that modern thought can devise. Over 2,500 years ago the Buddhists had already solved many of the problems that modern psychology is still discovering."

Francis Story, an English advocate of Buddhism, could not agree better when he says: "The doctrines of Buddha Dhamma stand today, as unaffected by the march of time and the expansion of knowledge as when they were first enunciated. No matter to what lengths increased scientific knowledge can extend man's horizon, within the framework of the Dhamma there is room for the acceptance and assimilation of further discovery."

There is no doubt that Buddhism has come to stay in the United States and has gradually gained public interest on many levels. Many American universities have programs of Buddhist studies up to the Ph.D. levels or include Buddhism as one of the subjects for academic pursuit in their religion-related departments. At the University of Wisconsin a program of Ph.D. Degree in Buddhist Studies has been established with the express aim "to train teachers and scholars to understand Buddhism not only as a datum of social or philosophical history but also as a profound expression of human religious experience, with ramifications in art, music, literature and the lives of its followers." Harvard University also offers facilities for Ph.D. students to pursue a program in the Study of Religion in the Special Field of Buddhism. Similar opportunities are also available at Columbia University where study in the special interdepartmental program on Buddhist subjects is worked out in conjunction with courses for a Ph.D. Degree.

With the interest and enthusiasm the Western world has shown in Buddhism and with our faith in the greatness and virtues of the Dharma, we have every reason to feel confident that the noble religion of the Buddha has taken permanent roots in the Western soil and it is only a matter of time for the roots to go deep.

QUESTIONS

PART I

Lesson 1

1. *What is Buddhism? Why are we called Buddhists?*
2. *How old is Buddhism? Where was it founded, and by whom?*
3. *Which country is known as the birthplace of Buddhism? Why?*
4. *Why is Buddhism respected by the intellectual?*
5. *Why do peace-loving people like Buddhist teachings?*

Lesson 2

1. *What are the objects of the highest veneration for Buddhists? What are they called collectively?*
2. *What are the three virtues of the Buddha?*
3. *What is the Dharma? How should we treat the Dharma?*
4. *What is the Sangha? Why do we respect it?*

5. *Explain how the Three Gems are interrelated.*

Lesson 3

1. *What does the word Buddha mean?*
2. *What are the Buddha's personal and clan names? By which name is he generally referred to?*
3. *Who were his parents? Where did they live?*
4. *When was Siddhattha born (give day, month, and year) and where?*
5. *What prediction did the eight Brahmins give for the infant prince?*

Lesson 4

1. *When did Queen Maya die? Who took care of young Siddhattha after that?*
2. *Describe Siddhattha's character in his early years.*
3. *What argument did Siddhattha present to win the injured bird from Devadatta ?*
4. *At what age and to whom was Siddhattha married?*
5. *What did Siddhattha's father want him to become?*

Lesson 5

1. *Was Siddhattha really satisfied with the condition of the world as he saw it? Why?*
2. *What did he see one day on his visit to the grove?*
3. *What effect did the sights have on Siddhattha?*
4. *What is the Great Renunciation?*
5. *How did the Great Renunciation benefit the world?*

Lesson 6

1. *Describe the kind of life Siddhattha led after the Great Renunciation.*
2. *Why was Siddhattha dissatisfied with the teachers he met?*
3. *What did he practice after he left those teachers?*
4. *How long did his search for the Truth take him? Who looked after him during that period?*
5. *On what day and at what age did Siddhattha attain enlightenment? How was he referred to after that?*

Lesson 7

1. *How did the Buddha discover the Truth (Dharma)? Who was his teacher?*
2. *Why did the Buddha at first hesitate to teach the Dharma? Why did he decide afterward to teach it?*
3. *When, where, and to whom did the Buddha deliver the first sermon?*

4. *What is the name of the first sermon? What does it symbolize? Explain in detail.*
5. *What does the first sermon explain?*

Lesson 8

1. *Who was the first person to perceive the truth after the Buddha?*
2. *What does the word "saṅgha" mean?*
3. *What are the two kinds of saṅgha? Explain.*
4. *Which invaluable service do the members of the Conventional Saṅgha perform?*
5. *Who was the first person to become a member of the Saṅgha?*

Lesson 9

1. *At what point did the Group of Five become completely enlightened (Arahant)?*
2. *What led Yasa to run away from his home?*
3. *What was the statement with which the Buddha aroused Yasa's curiosity?*
4. *How many monks did the Buddha have under him within the first year of teaching?*
5. *What was the statement with which the Buddha aroused the curiosity of the group of young men?*

Lesson 10

1. *How many years after the Buddha's enlightenment was the Order of nuns (bhikkhunī) established?*
2. *Who was the first Buddhist nun?*
3. *Who was the monk who persuaded the Buddha to create an Order of nuns? What was the argument that he used?*
4. *What made Bhaddā Kuṇḍalakesā tired of the world? How did she outwit her husband?*
5. *Who was the monk who defeated Bhaddā Kuṇḍalakesā in debate?*

Lesson 11

1. *Who was the king who supported the Buddha's teaching in the first few years?*
2. *Name two of the Buddha's most well-known disciples (not the Chief Disciples).*
3. *How did Anāthapiṇḍika buy Prince Jeta's grove?*
4. *What kind of people became the Buddha's disciples?*
5. *Is the Buddha's teaching specifically for monks and nuns?*

Lesson 12

1. *Who were the Buddha's two chief disciples?*
2. *Who was the Buddha's personal attendant for 25 years?*
3. *Who was the monk who memorized the Buddha's teachings?*
4. *Who was the monk who gave Sārīputta his first Buddhist teaching? Explain the teach-*

ing he gave.

5. *How did Moggallāna die? What was the bad karma he had committed?*

Lesson 13

1. *What was Aṅgulimāla's early name ? What does it mean?*
2. *Why did Aṅgulimāla take to the bandit's life?*
3. *What did Aṅgulimāla do with his victims? How many people did he kill?*
4. *Why did Aṅgulimāla's mother go to the jungle? What did Aṅgulimāla do when he saw his mother?*
5. *How did Aṅgulimāla, as a monk, win people's love and trust?*

Lesson 14

1. *Why did Paṭācārā run away from her family? Where did she go, and with whom?*
2. *Where did Paṭācārā have her first baby? Explain why and how she had it there?*
3. *Describe how Paṭācārā lost her husband and sons.*
4. *Why did Paṭācārā go mad? Describe her sufferings.*
5. *How did she recover from her insanity? Explain fully.*

Lesson 15

1. *Explain clearly how Siddhattha and Devadatta were related.*
2. *Describe the differences in Siddhattha's and Devadatta's characters.*
3. *Why did Devadatta eventually want to kill the Buddha?*
4. *Why did Devadatta befriend Ajātasattu?*
5. *What is mettā? Why and how should we develop it?*

Lesson 16

1. *How many years did the Buddha spend teaching the Dharma?*
2. *What were the Buddha's last words? Explain.*
3. *What is the term used to refer to the Buddha's prediction of his own death?*
4. *What was the request of the seven kings? What did they do when their request was turned down?*
5. *Who arranged the distribution of the Buddha's relics? How was it done?*

PART II

Lesson 1

1. *What is the meaning of "Vinaya Piṭaka"? What does it deal with?*
2. *Of the three Piṭakas, which is the most popular? Why?*
3. *Which is the most difficult Piṭaka? What does it contain?*

4. *What were the early Western views on Buddhism? Explain.*
5. *How did the West come to appreciate Buddhism?*

Lesson 2

1. *What are the two extremes the Buddha warned against?*
2. *What is the Middle Way? How many factors does it have and what are they?*
3. *Explain the Four Noble Truths in brief.*
4. *What happened to Koṇḍañña after the First Sermon?*
5. *Where was the First Sermon given?*

Lesson 3

1. *What does "dukkha" really mean? Give an explanation in your own words.*
2. *How many kinds of dukkha are mentioned in Buddhist philosophy? Write them out in Pali terminology.*
3. *What kind of dukkha is most apparent, and why?*
4. *Explain the second category of dukkha. Why are happiness and pleasure included in dukkha?*
5. *How is the third form of dukkha recognized and identified?*

Lesson 4

1. *Give a clear etymological explanation of the word "karma."*
2. *What is kusala-kamma? Give examples of kusala-actions.*
3. *What is akusala-kamma? Give examples of akusala-actions.*
4. *What are the ten unwholesome actions?*
5. *Give examples to demonstrate the positive aspect of wholesome actions.*

Lesson 5

1. *What is the meaning of "punabbhava"?*
2. *What is a "being" or an individual according to Buddhism? What does an individual consist of?*
3. *Why is it said that an individual is neither the same nor different for two consecutive moments?*
4. *What does the Law of Cause and Effect state with regards to rebirth?*
5. *Why should people always strive to do good and avoid evil?*

Lesson 6

1. *What is the meaning of Dhammapada? What does it contain?*
2. *What is the source of our actions? What is the result of a good action?*

3. *Describe the nature of the mind. Why should we train it?*
4. *Why did the Buddha say that evil people are their own enemies?*
5. *Why should a person be prompt to do good?*

Lesson 7

1. *What does the word "maṅgala" mean? Explain briefly.*
2. *Where was Maṅgala Sutta delivered, and why?*
3. *How many "blessings" are mentioned in Maṅgala Sutta? How are they graded ?*
4. *Whom should we associate with, whom should we avoid? Why?*
5. *What is the highest spiritual achievement in Buddhism? What is the nature of a person who has reached that state?*

Lesson 8

1. *What are the virtues leading to success, according to the Buddha? Name them with the Pali terms.*
2. *What is the first key to success? Explain why it is called the primary requirement.*
3. *How is the second virtue related to the first?*
4. *Explain how the third virtue is important for our success.*
5. *Describe the role of wisdom in the execution of one's work.*

Lesson 9

1. *What are the virtues that protect the world? Why are they so called?*
2. *How does a person practice hiri?*
3. *Explain the nature of hiri with examples.*
4. *How is ottappa developed; what belief gives rise to it? Explain in detail.*
5. *Explain the nature of Ottappa with examples. How does it effect one's character?*

Lesson 10

1. *What are the virtues necessary for material benefits in the present? Give the Pali terms and their English meaning.*
2. *Explain uṭṭhāna-sampadā. Illustrate your answer with suitable examples.*
3. *Why is ārakkha- sampadā necessary?*
4. *Explain how good friends or associates are important for a happy and successful life.*
5. *Demonstrate how a samajīvitā life is different from a non-samajīvitā one.*

Lesson 11

1. *Why is it said that mind is the forerunner of all actions, and why should we train our mind?*

2. *What is the difference between the trained and untrained mind?*
3. *Describe the benefits of Buddhist meditation.*
4. *What is the difference between Samatha- and vipassanā-bhāvanā?*
5. *What is the Satipaṭṭhāna Sutta? What does it teach?*

Lesson 12

1. *Where did the Great Demise take place?*
2. *How did the Buddha bear his illness?*
3. *Why did he subdue the illness and postpone his demise till a later time?*
4. *Did the Buddha appoint someone to take over the Order after him?*
5. *How old was the Buddha when he passed away?*

PART III

Lesson 1

1. *How does man rise above animal instinct? How does Buddhism help him?*
2. *Name a few things that the Buddha fought against. How does the religion free us from those evils?*
3. *How long did the Buddha's mission last? What do his discourses contain?*
4. *If we believe in the Buddha's advice to depend on ourselves, what effect will it have on us?*
5. *What is the best gift according to the Buddha? How can we share this gift with others?*

Lesson 2

1. *What are the things that Buddhists respect most?*
2. *What does it mean by "taking refuge in the Triple Gem"?*
3. *How does one take refuge in the Triple Gem? Is the presence of a Buddhist monk necessary?*
4. *What is the Confirmation Ceremony? Who usually officiates at the ceremony?*
5. *Translate the following:*
   Buddhaṁ saraṇaṁ gacchāmi
   Dutiyampi saṅghaṁ saraṇaṁ gacchāmi.
   Tatiyampi dhammaṁ, saraṇaṁ gacchāmi.

Lesson 3

1. *Why should a Buddhist practice his religion?*
2. *What are the objects a Buddhist respects most? What will happen if he rejects them?*
3. *How is one's faith in the religion strengthened?*
4. *What should be the attitude of a good Buddhist toward his parents?*

5. *Why should Buddhists be broad-minded in religious matters?*

Lesson 4

1. *What is worship as generally understood? Explain.*
2. *What is worship in Buddhism? What do we get from it?*
3. *Explain what we should and should not do while worshipping.*
4. *When we worship, what should we concentrate on? What should be strengthened in our hearts?*
5. *Translate: "Svākkhāto bhagavatā dhammo, dhammaṁ namassāmi."*

Lesson 5

1. *Why is the Buddha worthy of supreme veneration?*
2. *What does Buddhānussati mean? What is its practical use?*
3. *What is the meaning of "sandiṭṭhiko" and "ehipassiko"?*
4. *What is the primary role of the Sangha?*
5. *What is the meaning of "ujupaṭipanno bhagavato sāvakasaṅgho," "sāmīcipaṭipanno bhagavato sāvakasaṅgho," and "anuttaraṁ puññakkhettaṁ, lokassa"?*

Lesson 6

1. *What are the five precepts? What is the Pali word for the five precepts?*
2. *How does a person observe the five precepts? Is a monk absolutely necessary? Explain.*
3. *What do the second and the fourth precepts tell us to do?*
4. *What are the benefits of the five precepts? Write as much as you can understand from the lesson.*
5. *Explain the social implications of the third precept.*

Lesson 7

1. *Where is Thailand located? What is its population now, and what percentage of the population are Buddhist?*
2. *When did Buddhism come to Thailand? What is its status in the country today?*
3. *In what way do the rulers of the country support Buddhism?*
4. *What are the main sects of Buddhism now? To what sect does Thai Buddhism belong?*
5. *What do Buddhist monks generally do as a matter of duty and service to society?*

Lesson 8

1. *How many major Buddhist holy days are celebrated in Thailand? What are they? Do other countries celebrate them?*

2 *What is Māgha? What does Māgha Pūjā mean ?*
3. *What are the three principles of Buddhism?*
4. *When is the Visākha Pūjā Day? What is its significance?*
5. *What is the name of the first sermon, what does it signify?*

Lesson 9

1. *When did Buddhism first make contact with the West?*
2. *Who was the famous Indian Buddhist Emperor who ascended the throne in the year 218 B.E.?*
3. *Who founded the Pali text Society? What does the Society do?*
4. *How has Thailand contributed to teaching Buddhism in the West?*
5. *What other Buddhist countries have undertaken Buddhist activities in the West?*